LEFT HOME AT 16

by Frank Antilla

Doug:

12/17/2010

Life shrinks or expands
in proportion to one's Courage.

Frank Antilla

Dedicated to my three sons
Dean, Joe, and Scott Antilla.

Acknowledgements and appreciative thanks to Cheryl Reitan, for her constructive suggestions and direction; Samantha Lefebvre, for her story in a University of Minnesota Duluth paper. Gail Trowbridge, for her literary guidance; Mona Antilla Carloni, for designing the book cover, and Berdie Antilla, for 59 ½ years of patience, love and inspiration.

ISBN 978-0-578-07297-5

Printed and bound in the United States of America.

TABLE OF CONTENTS

Left Home at Sixteen

Preface

When the icy winds from the North sweep through our twelve acres and the nearby clearings and forests, stirring up the dust from the past seasons, as well as the memories from the past years, they move me to listen, sometimes into sleepless nights, for the sounds and the signs that remind one of the passing of time and people. So before I become a doddering old man, I am going to write about these ghost caravans of people and experiences.

My "life's highway" has been and continues to be, an interesting journey, encompassing good experiences, as well as some that were not. My early years were hard, mainly because of the loss of my father at an early age. On the other hand, by the time we pass the half century mark, most of us have had our share of slights, indignities or outright suffering. Perhaps it leads one to the serious contemplation of life and one's place in the universe. Is life worth living? Many of us have not found life worth living. One has to make it worth living.

Perhaps it was seeing my mother's determination; perhaps it was observing people in a challenging environment, people who not only survived, but went on to live lives of abundance, happiness and

stability; or perhaps it was the presence of God;
but whatever the factors were, I dreamed dreams
that were suggestive of a better life that led to goals,
that someday, I would be a winner, and those goals
sustained me, and gave me an advantage.

I am eighty-three years old. I survived and
succeeded. If I can do it, so can others. Hopefully, my
story will be interesting, and because of that, inspire
others—that regardless of one's early life experience,
we are life's master; the world cannot stop you.
Getting started is the first step. Go for it!

- Frank Antilla

Chapter 1
Born in North Dakota

I made my appearance on this earth in the state of North Dakota on a spring day in 1927. I remember it as a lonely, unfriendly prairie-land, with an incessant wind that blew most of the rich top soil to other more fortunate places. The undependable weather and the economy of the Great Depression of the 1930s, made mere existence and survival difficult.

In later years, anyone traveling through North Dakota would see vast areas of land littered with abandoned, decaying, broken homes, and farm buildings, visual evidence that for some immigrants, the promise of the American dream did not take place.

Regardless of these negative factors, immigrants from a myriad of foreign countries came in droves, among them my parents, Albert and Josephine Banttari Antilla from Finland. They came because they had heard that in America, land was free, to be given away, just for living and making improvements on it. This easy-to-understand and seemingly magical process even had a simple, inviting and easy-to-pronounce name: homesteading. Homesteading was a sharp departure from the antiquated, feudal-favored hierarchy of the old country, that made land ownership, security and the resulting happiness difficult, if not impossible, to obtain.

My parents came; fourteen of my brothers and sisters and I were born here. Ten of us survived. Five of the children passed on in their young years. The early demise of these five children left a six-year age difference between my siblings and me. I was the last child born and the youngest.

Chapter 2
The Ahola Cemetery

In August 1945, when I was a sailor in the Merchant Marine, I came home on leave. I drove my mother to North Dakota to a place where memories abounded, a place where, as a young girl, she became a bride, mother and homesteader.

While travelling through North Dakota, one becomes aware that because of the prairie, one can see for hundreds of miles in every direction. In the distance, on the side of a gradually sloping hill, we saw a smattering of tombstones. Near it was a small building for keeping people and their coffins during the winter months, when digging a hole in the frozen ground for their burial was too difficult, if not impossible.

Soon a faded rectangular sign came into view, next to an old worn road that led to the cemetery. Because of the passing of time and exposure to the harsh changing weather, the letters on the sign had faded and were barely discernible. With a little imagination, one could make out the word "Cemetery." The once flattened roadside grass, parched yellow by the drought, now stood straight. We could hear the faint sound of this grass brushing against the underside of the car as we drove the last quarter mile.

The Ahola Cemetery, an old Finnish graveyard, was a historical treasure. The ever-present prairie wind gave movement to the tall grass and the wildflowers, causing them to move and bend over the graves and brush against the tombstones and grave markers.

There was no sun, nor hint of a sun, even though there was not a cloud in the sky. A hawk like bird appeared, circled the area, finally landed on a tombstone in the outer boundaries of the cemetery, and looked in our direction. A lone horse was pawing at the dust in a nearby pasture. The wind had a lonesome sound or perhaps it only seemed lonesome, because of the absence of people, and we were left to our own thoughts of the past and the pictures that mother and I carried in our minds.

Mother pointed out the tombstone of my father and the graves of her deceased five children. I looked at her, the mother of fifteen children and the owner of a paralyzing cartload of memories. The seeds of sadness were sown throughout her life, but still a laugh was close to the surface.

Because of the lack of money, there were no tombstones for the children. Instead, there was improvisation, because that was life's necessity. At the time of her children's deaths, she had written each of their names on a sheet of store-bought tablet paper with the pertinent information: date of birth, date of baptism, date of death, and parents' names. She had then placed the notes in Kerr canning jars, closing the cover as tightly as she could. She placed each individual jar by the child's grave as the deaths occurred. Amazingly, the jars had survived and were still embedded in the ground.

I leaned over and carefully pulled one out of the ground, the glass aged and yellowed. It looked ancient and breakable. Over the years, the rain, snow, heat and cold had accelerated the aging process. I wiped the clinging strands of grass and weeds so that I could see the contents of the jar better. Many years had passed, but through the jar I could see wrinkled, yellowing, lined paper with my mother's primitive handwriting in the Finnish language.

Those glass canning jars seemed also to contain the experiences of those that have been here before us, filling us with sadness, amazement, and compassion. I remember saying to my mother, "The jars have survived for many years." She didn't speak; instead a deep sob rose up out of her. It was as if the vast accumulation of memories that had been bottled up finally sought release.

Years later, when I returned to the Ahola Cemetery with my wife Berdie, we bought a new tombstone with the five names engraved on it: Linda, Matti, Pekka, Veikko, and Jussi. They were the names of my sister and my four brothers. The canning jar grave markers were gone. They had served their purpose. We set the stone in the burial plot, next to my father's.

Chapter 3
The Prairie

Central North Dakota was a new land with challenges that created uncertainties, stress and unhappiness. Some of the challenges were insurmountable: rock-infested soil that lacked so many nutrients that it was almost sterile; severe winters and a short growing season; inadequate funds; an inability to converse and interact in the new strange English language; and the demands of large growing families. The immigrants came seeking solace and security, hoping to leave uncertainty behind.

My father found his respite from these uncertainties in strong drink. He discovered that alcohol could sweeten the caustic taste of failure, make the hills of life level, enhance his image of himself, and make life's journey pleasant and worth living, even for a short while. Regrettably, this alcoholic dream had a predictable, unhappy end. Because of his frequent escapes from the realities of life, my father became addicted to alcohol (sometimes made with questionable ingredients) and it finally led to his demise.

My mother lost her husband and my siblings and I, recently born, lost our father. My childhood and adolescent years were undoubtedly affected by my mother's maternal influence.

Because of the age difference between my siblings and myself, they had left home or were about to leave home when I came into the family. Because of this vacuum in the time element I missed the customary brother and sister interaction and relationship. As I grew up, they married and started families of their own or were working for their food and lodging elsewhere.

I lived with my mother in an old wood frame house, a vast improvement from the sod house that my parents built and lived in for most of their married life. This wood frame house was cold in the winter and hot in the summer. It was also inherent with unexplainable sounds and noises, especially on windy days which gave my mother an opportunity to use her clever, grim and often ironic humor to entertain herself, her little boy or anyone else who happened to be there.

One stormy night the house was rampant with noises of all sorts. Boards and wood creaked as the old house leaned with the gusting wind that was blowing through clumps of bushes and tall prairie grass, and into cavities, cracks in the aging boards. At the same time, the wind created music like sound effects and mysteriously alternating in intensity causing the lamp to flicker ominously.

I was peering out the window into the dark stormy night, and fearfully asked my mother, "Mikka se anni ulkona on?" ("What is that sound outside?") My mother replied with a humorous, yet serious look on her face, "Se on Wainio's leski senn kairrvutt ja hevosit menne sivuten." ("That is widow Wainio's wagon and horses going by.")

So I stared into the stormy darkness expecting to see the tall, gaunt figure of widow Wainio dressed in her old, worn clothing with a large piece of rag cloth wrapped tightly around her head and shoulders and the leather reins of her horses clutched tightly in her worn, calloused hands. But alas! I could not see Widow Wainio, yet she must have been out there because my mother said so. Poor Mrs. Wainio. I hoped she would survive. She did survive, because she was not out there. All that was out there was a black North Dakota night, a stormy, gusty wind and sand storm with sound effects.

This was an introduction to a young boy of his mother's wry humor and thought-provoking conversations. She made statements that had to be thought about in order to derive their true meaning. They were always lessons related to daily living or life.

Chapter 4
Matt Maki

Eventually, a personable smiling man by the name of Matt Maki moved into our home. He was a musician, carver, philosopher and story teller. In this day and age, when a man moves in with a woman, it would be called "shacking up" or "living together." I was too young to discern the propriety of this relationship. All I knew is that our home now had more talk and laughter. I wistfully thought of calling him father, but I did not dare . . . yet.

Matti played a button accordion and carved wooden spoons out of pieces of birch wood that he carried in his pack sack. The birch wood was easily attainable for it grew readily alongside roads in nearby Minnesota.

I watched his competence with a carving knife as he whittled his wood spoons. I appreciated and admired his talent as he played Finnish music on his button accordion in a minor key, which gives it an Eastern mystical flavor, that even now, when hearing music that is similar, my inner chemistry is aroused, making me wonder about the connection between music, consciousness and the past.

Matt's presence gave our home balance and pleasure.

If someone had told me that Matt had hung the moon, I would have believed that person.

I would not let Matt out of my sight. It was almost like having a father. The feeling was not reciprocated or appreciated by Matt. Matt soon let it be known that he was not in our home to be a surrogate father. He was in our home for a more basic reason, a relationship with a woman who was my mother. One day, my elusive father-fantasy crashed. Matt made his customary trip to our outhouse with me following close behind. He went inside and I remained outside waiting.

After what seemed like a long time, I called out in the loudest voice that I could muster, "Isa on hysikassa pitkan aika."("Father is in the toilet a longtime.") Soon after, Matti came out of the outhouse, his usual smiling face contorted with irritation and anger. He looked down at me and said, "Ala kuutsu minua sinun isaksi. Enn mina aleh sinun isa." ("Don't call me your father; I am not your father.") The sting that I experienced was followed by unbelief, silence and hurt.

The relationship between my mother and Matt progressed until one day, Matt and my mother left me with my oldest brother Arnie and his family, and then departed. Eventually, their relationship ended and my

13

mother came home and picked up her three-year-old son and life continued.

Some twenty years later, I was a wheelsman on an ore boat that had docked in Superior, Wisconsin, a town where my brother Arthur lived. Being off watch, I went ashore and stopped in at Arthur and his wife Mary's house and they had company.

Arthur asked me, "You remember Matt Maki don't you?" "Yes," I replied after recovering from shock of seeing this man from the distant past, my thoughts racing back over the years. "I remember Matti!"

Silently I thought of the time that Matt came out of the outhouse and my greeting to him. I looked at this aged man, in worn, wrinkled clothes, a man who had hurtled through life and relationships with women. When I was growing up, there was an excess of women and scarcity of responsible men because of the sociology of that time period. Men died in dangerous work, became victims of alcoholism, returned to the old country, committed suicide, or left for other foreboding reasons. Due to these circumstances, many women become willing participants in unmarried relationships.

Matt showed no signs of recognizing me that day. Too many years of marginal living, too many experiences life had meted out, had erased the unimportant memory of a three-year-old boy who had insisted on calling him father, an appellation that he did not want or relish. Now, the little boy was no longer little. He had ceased to be the shattered, fatherless little boy who so desperately wanted to call him father eons ago.

Matt was no longer the youthful, confident ladies' man of years gone by, a man who had had no time for little boys searching for a father figure. Looking at his face, a feeling of compassion surged up in me, for I remembered a joyous person, in the prime of life, full of vitality and manhood. Now I was looking at an old man with deep lines on his face, lines that indicated a life of bitter struggles, pinched, worn and tremulous. To watch him was painful. After some small talk and a courteous short visit, I bade him goodbye. In return, he gave me a halfhearted look of indifference.

I was glad to get away. As we get older, we say a final goodbye to a lot of people. I returned to my ship and got ready to go on watch. That night while steering the ship, and staring into an illuminated compass, I silently reenacted my visit with Matt Maki. A significant visit indeed. That night sleep did not come easily.

Chapter 5
Farming

Through hard work and grit, my mother continued farming the homestead and raised a sizeable herd of beef cattle. Her oldest son was married with a growing family, hard pressed for money. Aware of his mother's growing herd of beef cattle, he mortgaged his mother's livestock without her knowing about it. Regrettably, he was unable to pay the loan back before the due date.

Thus, bankers came out, riding in a fine car, one of them carrying a briefcase with important looking documents. They were followed by many cattle trucks with their high, sturdy wood side-boards, designed for hauling animals. The banker explained to my mother the details of her son's loan and informed her that they were now going to take possession of the cattle and load them up into the waiting trucks. My mother told the bankers in broken English and Finnish, "You can't do that." The banker replied, "The cattle are mine, and I will take them. If I don't, your son will go to jail." The men took most of the herd.

Shortly after this, my mother made arrangements to move to Minnesota with her family. She paid for this move with the few cattle and horses that she managed to keep.

Chapter 6
On to Minnesota

It was on to Minnesota and a new life. A life that
was basic: food, shelter, and warmth. We moved
into an old log building deep in the forest, miles
from neighbors and a challenging two-day round
trip by horse and sled to several small towns. The log
building was owned by an old sinewy Finn named
Sakkri Thermos, who traveled swiftly through the
woods on homemade cross country skis and a pack
sack on his back.

It was said that he was an inveterate gambler. He
managed to win enough money to sustain him in
his meager and spartan way of life. He returned to
the cabin periodically on his home skis. While at
the cabin, he would go into the woods and cut strips
of bark off certain trees and boil the bark in water
on the wood stove. He'd drink the beverage that he
said would cure anyone of whatever ailed them and
guarantee a long and vigorous life.

My mother and I lived by ourselves. One sister, Saima
Dagmar, had gotten married at the age of sixteen,
and my other sister Gertrude and older brother
Oscar found homes where they could work for their
room and board and also go to school.

Occasionally, every couple weeks or so, my mother would harness Nikki, our long-legged horse. This was difficult because of my mother's short stature. She would grab the harness, step up on a milk stool, lift the harness and throw it over the horse toward its head. She would then go to the other side of the horse and catch hold of some part of the harness and pull it downward and cinch up the buckles and straps.

She would hitch up the horse to a horse sled, pull off the tarp covering that protected the sled that was filled with dry hay. We snuggled ourselves into the hay, covered ourselves with a homemade blanket, and left on our journey through the forest to go visiting. It was seven to ten miles to the nearest neighbor, almost a day's journey one way.

One of the several neighbors' homes that we visited was Isac and Hilda Mattson. When we arrived at the Mattson's, Isac would come out and unhitch the horse, take it to the barn, take the harness off, and feed the horse fresh hay. Mother and I were warmly received with immediate coffee and lunch and a request to stay overnight or for a longer visit. The Mattson's were generous and warm-hearted. We enjoyed their hospitality, hearty food, warm house, laughter and much conversation in the Finnish language.

When our visit coincided with "sauna night" which was on Saturdays, neighbors would walk over from nearby farms to have a sauna and a visit. Hilda Mattson would bake pastries and rolls that the visitors would enjoy after their saunas.

Couple by couple or family by family, they would take turns going to the sauna building, while others would drink their coffee and contribute to the flow of community news, gossip and conversation. Isac had piles of wood and a well close to the sauna and as the people finished their sauna, the man or woman would make sure that the stove had adequate wood and the water replenished in the barrels for the others that would be using the sauna that night.

Chapter 7
Songs & Pennies

It happened that during these sauna and neighborhood visitation nights, people would notice me, Fransi, a shy little boy close to my mother and they would speak to me. Though I was close-lipped, I would respond in Finnish. One day, a friendly warmhearted old Finn addressed me. He said, "Fransi, if you would sing us a song, I will give you a penny." It just so happened that I had memorized a song I had learned in first grade.

The thought of earning a penny in the early 1930s, overcame my fear of standing before a group, so I walked to the center of the room, took a deep breath and at the top of my lungs, let go with this little ditty, which I will never forget. "Jack and Jill went over the hill to fetch a pail of water; Jack fell down and broke his crown and Jill came tumbling after."

The people enjoyed this performance immensely, and thus unknowingly a little boy had started a neighborhood social custom that was entertaining and refreshing: singing songs for pennies. It was entertainment and a brief departure, from cares and deprivations. Eventually, I was requested to leave any outside activity with other kids and come into house to sing a song, I would always oblige, because the pennies were accumulating and sometimes I received two or three pennies or a whole nickel or a dime. Wow!

Once a man asked me to sing a song before a group of visiting neighbors at his home. I had my usual response, "I will, if you give me a penny." So I sang and when I walked over to his chair for payment, he looked into his leather money bag. These bags were carried by all men to keep their change and paper money and were of a size that would fit into a trouser pocket. There were no credit cards or driver's licenses then, so a leather bag functioned very well.

After looking into his bag, he could not find any pennies. I felt cheated. I thought, I would never forget this incident or person. Weeks later, the same man asked me to sing a song for a penny. I said, "I will if you pay me a penny and also a penny for the last time that I sang for you." My response caused the room to fill with laughter. I sang a song, and then the man brought over a handful of pennies, patted me on the head, and recited the old Finn saying: "Hyva poika." (Good boy.)

My growing accumulation of pennies and other coins gave me an enjoyable way to entertain myself. I liked to take the bank apart and spread the coins out on a homemade quilt. I examined each one, enjoying the feel of the coins. It was real money. Wow! I arranged them in stacks and counted them again before returning the coins to the bank.

My bank was made of heavy metal in the shape of a horse. The name "Black Beauty" was written in raised letters on the horse's side. It was a bank that earlier had been empty and used as a toy horse in a little boy's imaginative fantasy and games.

The bank became functional, for what it was intended, a place that you could stuff money into. The horse-bank did not offer any security because it only consisted of two pieces of metal held together by a screw. It was small enough to easily fit into one's pocket.

Regrettably some unknown person came and removed the screw that held the two halves together and stole the pennies, nickels and dimes and left an empty bank. It was an unbelievable happening, because little boys are basically honest. Learning to be dishonest comes later in life.

It taught me the lesson that we are all inherently flawed and vulnerable to do wrong, and that is what it means to be human. It still hurts after all those years. This was the beginning of the years of

Depression, a period of time when stealing became in some cases a necessity, tempting and prevalent. Four or five dollars taken in a dishonest way, from a little boy, apparently outweighed the morality of this degrading behavior. We must forgive our debts as we forgive our debtors.

Chapter 8
Mrs. Koivu

From our woods cabin, we moved to a small, cheaply built dwelling. Our new home was closer to neighbors, but a visit to the closest town was a well-planned event because of the distance. Our life centered around our sparse resources. Limitations were always present. Our new home kept out the elements, but barely. As I look back, my good fortune was mother's courage, and determination. As money was needed, mother had sold Nikki, our favorite horse as well as the remaining horses and cattle that had been hauled from North Dakota.

Whenever we had to go somewhere, we walked. Unknowingly, we were experiencing a healthy way of life that included eating from the garden, walking, gathering fallen firewood from the nearby forest, and other improvisations that required physical activity. Our lifestyle kept us healthy, as well as made us strong.

We had a neighbor directly across the road from our place. Even though this happened in the 1930s, for the sake of anonymity and possible embarrassment, I will call her Mrs. Koivu.

My mother and Mrs. Koivu had a testy relationship.
Mrs. Koivu was a widow. Her deceased husband
had been successful and because of this, when he
passed on, he was able to provide for his widow and
one son with what would be considered an ample
estate. Because of her wealth, attractive demeanor,
and verbal skills, Mrs. Koivu had many suitors.
Inquisitiveness, a human trait, and talk in the
community's ladies groups contributed to further
interest in Mrs. Koivu's life and her comings and
goings.

Mrs. Koivu did not have any control over the stories
about her life, causing her resentment to grow. My
mother had a small window that faced Mrs. Koivu's
home, so Mrs. Koivu may have reasoned that my
mother was the informant. Mrs. Koivu had a large
bay window that faced our home, and the country
road was used by the traveling inquisitive world. As
she gazed at our small house, anger and vindictive
plans began to formulate.

Mrs. Koivu went on the offensive. At social
gatherings like funerals, stores or even an unlikely
place like a shoe repair shop, Mrs. Koivu would put
on an Academy Award-winning snub. If the occasion
presented itself, she would deliver a few cutting
words about the poor people in our community,
possibly accompanied by the darkest insult one

could give to a Finn, which was to suggest that their poverty was brought on by lack of activity, commonly known as laziness.

My mother, proud Josephine Antilla, felt the accumulation of this degradation had reached its limits. One day, an opportunity presented itself for my mother to show Mrs. Koivu what she was made of.

Mr. Makela, one of Mrs. Koivu's more frequent men friends, paid her a visit. Because of the thin uninsulated walls in our small home, one could easily hear noisy automobiles. Mrs. Koivu saw my mother watching her house through her small window, and Mrs. Koivu thought up a plan to damage Josephine's ego and put her where she belonged—in a subordinate place of embarrassment forever.

But the timing had to be precise in order for it to be effective. When Mrs. Koivu saw or surmised that Josephine was at her little window again, she quickly backed up her derriere against her large bay window, raised her dress, leaned over far enough to cause her derriere to be completely exposed and wiggled it from side to side, making it easier for any observer to detect the movement and the message that was being conveyed in such an unorthodox, creative as well as demeaning manner, to the intended recipient,

Josephine. But Mrs. Koivu underestimated the tenacity of her feisty neighbor.

Meanwhile, Josephine gathered her wits. As she was limited by her small window, she strode out into her yard, where no saplings or brush would block the view and take away from the command performance that she was about to give. Josephine turned her back to Mrs. Koivu's house, lifted up her homemade, dress exposing her pink Montgomery Ward bloomers, and made a majestic bow to the forest, while at the same time exposed her back end and underwear to Mrs. Koivu at her bay window and any cars that happened to be chugging by on that isolated country road.

This relationship did improve, perhaps because of the unspoken and hidden admiration that Josephine and Mrs. Koivu had for each other; one rich, the other poor, but both proud, strong willed and unwilling to concede defeat.

Chapter 9
Bovey

Shortly after this incident, my mother decided to move to the Iron Range town of Bovey. Bovey was typical of iron mining range towns. The towns had a smattering of many ethnicities. These ethnic groups were not ashamed of their recent European background. A trip to the Iron Range was like a mini-trip to Europe.

People on the streets chattered away unabashedly in foreign languages. Grocery stores of various ethnicities abounded. The Italians had Coppoletti's where garlic-loaded, fly-covered salami hung in smoke-smudged windows facing the street. It seemed as if clean windows might take away the mystique of an already busy store.

The Finns had their mercantile store, "Merk" where hard-sugared toast and coffee breads were available, the Serbians had Dimiche's and succulent sausages. The Swedes had Hageman's with robust, old country rye bread.

Then there were smoke-filled saloons where hard liquor and beer were served. Conversations took place in the speakers' native tongue, which resulted in a variety of languages, interlaced with words like "sonovabeetch" and "bassturrd." It was interesting to note that, profanity, swearing and four-letter words were reserved for the English language.

These saloons were also characterized by many parts of Europe. The Serbian's had Big Dan's, the Italian's had Coppoletti's, the Finns had Puuras, the Greek's had Pantages, the Polish had Novelty Lunch, the Slovanian's had Palm Gardens, the Turkish had Turkey Jim's, the Irish had Whitmas Hotel and the Austrian's had Spechts.

Miners, lumberjacks, people of all nationalities bellied up to the bar, at all hours, day and night, loud juke-box music such "San Antonio Rose" and "The Beer Barrel Polka" spilling out into the streets. It was inviting for marginal drinkers to forget their senses, enter, indulge and get to a state of drunkenness and perhaps a visit to one of the rooms in at least several of the taverns, where surreptitiously, ladies were working at the world's oldest profession.

The saloons were a place of bliss where regrets, aching bodies, undesirable workplaces, low wages, and other cares and responsibilities pleasantly faded away, even for a few hours.

Chapter 10
Friends

The little Iron Range village of Bovey was part of my awakening to another world. Bovey was an eye-opening and fearful place to me, the new kid on the block, and a first grader at that. At first, I crawled through the grass like an Indian scout to watch older boys playing baseball. I viewed them quietly and backed out carefully day after day, until I felt it was safe to walk upright to the group and hopefully find a friend. There were a lot of boys to play with and after getting beat up once in a while and also after winning a skirmish or two, I began to fit in.

John Moroni, a neighbor boy of Italian descent, came from a family situation that was similar to mine. I had lost my father and he had lost his mother. His father was raising a family of five—two girls and three boys—by himself. John and his brothers were among the kids with whom I went to school, played, fought, and grew up.

There was an isolated area behind the Bovey School where the janitors dumped the cinders from the school furnace. It was an area that we walked through on our way to and from school. It was also the place where John and I would get into our fights. I learned that the best strategy in any encounter was to lead with my left and punish with my right and keep a slim profile and thus a smaller target for his blows.

We had several fights which I won. I was becoming confident with my ability to defend myself because I had learned how to win over John, who was as tough as he looked, and instinctively ruled the roost in kid's play. His tough look and reputation was a definite deterrent for any confrontations.

In one of our back-of-the-school, cinder-pile fights, I walked into John's stiff left fist and felt a crushing blow from his right. I saw stars and experienced dizziness and a spinning world, besides shame and a deep hurt. I was down and beaten! This happened early in the day. That day in school, my defeat and disbelief that I had been beaten soundly occupied my thoughts.

I was so lost in my thoughts that I had not noticed John all day, until I found him blocking a doorway that I had to go through to get to another class. The confident look on his face, bordering on brashness, seemed to say that in my defeat I had given him the secret of life. That look did it for me, instinctively and intuitively. I practically shouted at him, "You'll never do that again, you wop son-of-a bitch-Moroni. Meet me at the cinder pile after school."

So, with the Bovey School as a back drop, we met on the cinder pile. Standing on the sooty cinders, staring into one another's eyes, each one of us, trying to stare the other one down into fear and defeat affected my fighting abilities. We were two young kids, both from a life of deprived circumstances, both with Iron Range citizenry in our blood lines. We probably both felt fear and courage, and we went at it. I did my best, but John did it again. Two times in one day. I was badly beaten, physically and inwardly. I didn't realize it at the time, but physical encounters at my young age, provided conditioning for survival in future years.

Chapter 11
My 65¢ Wagon

One day, I was sauntering through a Bovey alley with Ralph and Doamie Johnson. As usual, we were looking for something to catch our interest, be it mischief, putting a few coins in our pockets, or finding something that was happening, anything that was a departure from the uneventful hot summer days of life in a small iron range village. Lo and behold, there it was: Harold Koski emptying and rearranging long-stored items from a building facing the alley.

In those days, fifty years seemed like eternity to a young boy. Now to the same boy, a fifty-year time span doesn't seem that long. Boxes, books, and other aged, faded items, littered the Koski backyard. Some of them had been in storage a half century. In earlier years, recycling was a way of life. Wear it, look at it, use it, but never throw it away.

Among these aged items sat an old wooden wagon with heavy iron wheels. A handle attached to the front wheels could be used for pulling. If pushed back over the wooden box, one would use it for steering when coasting down hills. The old well-kept wagon was an oddity, because it had the appearance that it was built to last forever and unique, because it was the only one around and caught the attention of the young and the old.

The heavy, solid iron wheels caught my attention. They would be noisy on the cement sidewalks, no doubt, but the combined weight of four iron wheels would make the wagon fast for coasting down hills. To us, a speedy fast wagon was almost like owning an automobile. It looked more and more like a good deal. I could picture myself careening down King Hill, loaded with kids, and me the pilot with the steering handle in my hands. What a fantasy.

Just then the owner came into view. Trying to keep my excitement contained and my voice indifferent, I nonchalantly asked, "Hey Harold, what will you take for that ancient wagon over there?" He thought for a moment, somewhat taken back for this unexpected interest in this old relic that was probably manufactured before World War I. "Tell you what, you can have it for six bits," he said.

I put on my thinking cap. Let see, I have twenty cents, I thought. It was a rare occasion for me to have this much money. I ran down to see my sister Gertrude, who worked as a waitress in a local eatery, she gave me another twenty cents. I then went and stole two milk bottles off Mrs. Perttila's porch, and redeemed them for a nickel a piece. I went and begged my mother for a quarter. She gave me fifteen cents. I now had a total of sixty five cents.

All of this was accomplished in less than forty-five minutes. I ran down to Harold Koski's back yard, and practically shouted, "I'll tell you what, Harold. I'll give you sixty-five cents for that old wagon."

"Take it away," he replied.

Excited and eager, the three of us took the wagon and headed for King Hill and our test run. Future employment: test pilots for Lockheed Aircraft, we fantasized.

King Hill bordered one side of the rectangular perimeter of the small village of Bovey. Highway 169 and the main street were on the opposite side of town. Therefore, the location of the hill was ideal for clandestine forms of fun, like a noisy wagon with iron wheels and rough and unsafe-appearing planks, makeshift wheels, cut-off broom handles, and a metal pot cover screwed on the end for a steering wheel that was thrust through a used orange crate, nailed onto the plank. An old borrowed clothesline, wrapped around the broom handle leading to the steering wheel completed the steering mechanism of a "soap box derby" contender. And it worked. Maybe there were other more conventional forms of "fun coasting rigs," but there was only one wood wagon with iron wheels.

About two-thirds of King Hill was very steep, with the remaining third just the right distance to slow down your wagon, scooter, soapbox rig or whatever, before you reached the main traffic-filled street.

We got to the top of King, and the three of us easily fit into the wagon's wooden box. The wagon immediately started to move and gain momentum. When the iron wheels ran over the cracks on the sidewalk, the staccato, clanking noise became more pronounced.

About in the middle of the hill, we were still gaining momentum. At the crossover where the various streets joined King Hill, the terrain was slightly elevated and had a slight accumulation of gravel and small pebbles, leftover from sandings over the previous winter. Our wagon became slightly airborne as we flew over the road and gravel, and clattered back onto the narrow sidewalk. The ensuing sounds from the iron wheels caused a sense of wonderment in the small town. What is happening on King Hill?

Faster and faster, hanging onto the steering handle, I started thinking, what if a car darted out from any of the streets leading to King Hill? People that lived on or close to the hill, started coming out of their homes to see what was happening. They got a fleeting glimpse of three young boys careening down King Hill, two of them hanging on for dear life and the third boy intent on steering the wagon as it went rattling by at highway speeds on a bumpy sidewalk. As the hill leveled, the wagon lost its momentum, but the occupants did not lose their enthusiasm. It was only the beginning of fun on summer vacation.

Unknown to us three boys, our noisy wagon was creating a disturbance to some who lived on the hill. We found this out on ensuing rides. On one of our rides, a middle-aged woman appeared, crouched in an unfriendly attack stance, fists filled with small stones and gravel. It was the kerchiefed, scowling, blockish, and square body of Maara Swetich, her dark Slavic features contorted in anger as she shouted at our approaching, noisy, speeding wagon. She shouted at us, "My Steve workka nighttaa sheefta. He gotta sleeppaa. Go onna hoamaa Keets, or I keela yew. Yew heera watt I say, yess?" She then flung her handfuls of small rocks and gravel as we sped by.

This hostile action deterred us from any further rides that day. Unknown to Maara Swetich, however, dodging her stones and gravel, watching her angry Slav face shout threats and obscenities at us only added to the excitement of a wild ride down King Hill. Besides the speed of the wagon, we now had new challenges on our King Hill flight. Looking back, my regrets to Steve for disturbing his rest on his night shift schedule, even though the ride, the wagon, and Maara Swetich remain a fun memory.

Chapter 12
A Job

Money has always been an important commodity. People had very little, and my mother had less. I thought, if only I could get some kind of a job. I could buy a candy bar, or perhaps a bottle of pop or even a milk shake like a few other kids that had working fathers.

Sometime around 1936, I went to every merchant in town and asked each one of them at least every six weeks or so the same question: "You don't happen to have a little job that I could do around your business?" It was easy for them to respond with "I don't."

Finally, I lucked out; the town photographer, Erick Enstrom (who later gained fame for taking the classic photograph "Grace.") gave me a promising response. "I will have a job for you, if and when Autie Jacobson quits. If that ever happens, I will let you know." Sometime later, he came over to our home and let me know that Autie Jacobson had just quit and got a part time job at Lehrols gas station, a step up from the job he had at Enstrom's.

I reported to work after school with my heart in my mouth and eagerness and excitement in my gut. Mr.

Enstrom showed me how to go into his dark room and empty the discarded photography paper, go upstairs to Enstrom's apartment home and empty the house waste containers, carry the darkroom and the apartment waste to a garbage can located in the alley, close to the outside firewood building, and into another building on the far side of their lot and chop pieces of birch and other hardwood into sizes that would fit into Mrs. Enstrom's upstairs cook stove.

I'd chopped enough wood to fill the large wood box, carried the chopped wood from the outside building upstairs to the box. In addition, I chopped a small amount of kindling just in case the fire had to be restarted. That would be six days a week. Saturday's work could be done early in the day, because there was not any school that day.

I asked Mr. Enstrom, "How much will I be paid?"

"Twenty-five cents a week," he replied. That was a disappointment indeed! It was better than nothing and I reasoned that if I did a good job, a raise might be forthcoming. It was inspiring to have an income, even if it was only a quarter a week.

After working at Enstrom's for a month or so, Erick Enstrom called me into the studio one day, and asked me how the new job was going. Taken by surprise, I wondered if the inquiry could lead to something good, like more wages. Optimist that I was, I replied, "Fine, but I believe the job should pay more than a quarter a week."

"Vell wott do you tank yew shuut be pait," he asked in a great Swedish accent with its alternating tonal pitch. I decided to go for broke. "At least a dollar and a half a week." Mr. Enstrom paled at my response. "Vell I tell yuu vaat, I vill taak itt ohfer wit my eldest sohn Raajer, and I vill laet yuu know."

Several weeks went by, and Erick Enstrom told me that I would now be receiving a ten-cent raise. Thirty-five cents a week, instead of twenty-five cents.

Money in the mid-1930s was scarce and earned with difficulty. I decided not to waste it. I forgot about my earlier longings for pop and candy, No siree! I would walk by those stores that sold the large bottles of Hires Root Beer for a nickel. No way was I going to waste my money on something that I could eat or drink in several minutes and then my money was gone forever. I wanted something of permanence, of value.

I had been looking at a pair of hickory skis in Magerlie Brothers Hardware Store. They were priced at $7.50. They had a leather strap and buckle that went through the ski in the foot area.

The skier would then improvise with an inch wide rubber band cut from a discarded car tire inner tube. All car tires had inner tubes in those days. One would put this band of rubber over his shoe and in the ankle area, like putting on a pair of socks. Then you would put your shoe into the opening on the leather strap of the ski and take and stretch the rubber band over the toe of the shoe and then release it. Once you did this on both skis, the rubber band would do a wonderful job of keeping your shoes from slipping off the skis as you went striding through the woods, with ski poles flying. The poles were made out of saplings, the same length as the height of the skier.

All you had to do was push alternately with the right and then left poles and at the same time thrust your body forward and glide. It was a coordinated effort with the arms, legs, skis and poles. It was fun, a great physical sport that often gave the skier a psychological "high," when the outing was long and strenuous. The snow-covered waste dumps of the mining companies, as well as the hills and fields were free to use.

I needed a new pair of skis, because all I had were a pair of old pine skis I had inherited from brother Oscar. Pine skis warp easy. When a ski warps, it wants to deviate from going straight, causing you to turn at inopportune time. This unexpected turning would cause the skier to fall when thrusting forward, and also cause falls on home-made ski jumps. At high speeds, falling was a constant possibility.

I went to the hardware store and told the owner that I wanted to buy the skis in the front window. I wanted to buy the skis on the time-payment plan. I had saved up one dollar and fifty cents, which I would pay down, and then I would pay the balance of six dollars at thirty-five cents a week. After all, I was an 11 year old that had to learn responsibility.

Mr. Magerle answered, "I'll tell you what, it will take you over four months to pay the balance and it will be well into spring by then. I will take your $1.50 and you can pay off the balance each week and you take the skis with you and use them."

"No," I said, "I am afraid I would break them before I got them paid for, and then it would be difficult to continue paying for a broken pair of skis." It was finally agreed that I pay a dollar and a half down and pay thirty five cents a week, until the unpaid balance was amortized. So as it happened, when I finally got the skis paid for, the snow was gone, but I was elated and proud, for I now had a new, completely paid for skis, for the coming winter, and winters to come.

Erik Enstrom

Chapter 13
Poverty

The years went by. They were not entirely happy years because I had an older brother who was an alcoholic. He had a government-funded job through the W.P.A. (Works Progress Administration.) This job was given to him and to others that were unemployed. He got the job, but it was contingent on supporting our mother and me. Regrettably, most of his meager wages were spent on his drinking habit. As a result, there was hardly enough money for rent and food, let alone clothes or any extras for my mother and myself.

My clothes were old, and patched countless times. My winter coat was an old wool army coat that had been taken apart and recut into smaller pieces and then resewn to fit a smaller body by my mother, who was adept in sewing patches on trousers, but sewing and tailoring a winter coat required more sewing skills than she had. The coat did not fit well. The mittens from the same material did not look that great, but they kept me warm and humble.

Improvisation in clothing cost me the taunts and jeers of classmates. My boots were purchased in a larger size so that they would continue to fit my feet several years later. Even though my body and my limbs grew larger and longer, the out-sized boots continued to fit. One problem that had to be solved is that as I was an active boy, the leather soles quickly wore through, creating a hole in the center of the sole. The hole then let in moisture, pebbles, sticks and anything smaller than the hole.

Ingenuity and creativity took care of the soles. Old newspapers were folded and refolded into a rectangular shape the size of the boot's sole and then stuffed into the inside of each boot. The newspaper inserts had to be replaced every day, because the newspaper would disintegrate into smaller pieces in a few hours. On rainy days they had to be replaced more often. The heels eventually wore down or dropped off. By then, the boots were well-worn and ready for replacement.

I contributed further to this "wretched poor boy appearance" by my own misadventures, like getting my new, permanent front teeth knocked out. Me and the other kids played water spraying games with an old portable potato sprayer. When it was my turn, I filled the sprayer with water, pumped the sprayer full of pressurized air by pushing on a rod with handle on top of sprayer tank, and let out one cold squirt that shot out fifteen to twenty feet. This required a lot of pumping and pressure.

The pump handle had to be turned a quarter turn to prevent the pressurized air from leaking out. It had to be turned in the right direction; otherwise it would fly upward with force. I heard the hissing of escaping air and turned the handle in what I thought was the right direction to stop it.

It was the wrong direction, and the pump handle flew up with force and knocked my front teeth out. Trauma indeed! I told the other kids not to tell anyone with difficulty, because of the pain and the blood gushing out of my mouth. After that, I remember I made an effort to look more serious and smile less often because of my missing teeth.

My haircuts, which were given by my mother, were something to be desired. In ill-fitting, makeshift clothes, haircuts and missing teeth, I was wounded, but not beaten. I had become an honor student in the "school of hard knocks" in growing up in Bovey. Then we moved eleven miles further north.

Chapter 14
Lawrence Lake

Around 1938, we moved into a house on Lawrence Lake. The lake was approximately four miles long. The width of the lake varied. Near our home, it was approximately six city blocks wide. The lake was a source of interest, enjoyment, and lastly, a source of food. I regard the three to four years that we lived there, the happiest time of my younger years.

The lake seemed to have a human-like personality. One day, it was like a lake on the cover of a magazine printed for the tourist industry, bubbling over with inviting waves, the water matching color with the blue skies overhead, lofty towering pine tree casting their shadows on the pristine shoreline, and bringing on feelings of well being and good times.

The next day might bring change, a different image for the viewer, with gusty winds, a dark, glowering, and vindictive sky, that helps to bring on that unwholesome human condition of melancholia, despair and loneliness—a condition that characterized the economic depression on the Iron Range as well as the rest of the country.

The house we moved into on Lawrence Lake was a

story and a half wood frame building, with peeling white paint, inside and out. It was built by an immigrant who possessed few coins in his purse and fewer carpenter skills. The home had been adequate to meet his simple needs and the low rental fees were in alignment with my mother's sparse resources.

My room was upstairs. The builder scrimped on building materials, most notably in the upstairs, an area that would not be seen by many. Only minimal boards were used; just enough to keep the elements outside. I could easily hear the sounds emanating from the outside world: the whine of the wind, the sounds of the birds, and the power of the waves on Lawrence Lake. Just lying in bed and listening to the sounds activated my senses to along with my imaginative mind. I felt a closeness to nature.

"Poika, se on aika noesta ylis" ("Boy, it is time to get up.") With that I jumped up; grabbed my cut-off overall pants and put them on; bounded down the stairs three, four steps at a time; ran through a couple of rooms to the back door; pushed open the screen door, and while still on the run, gave another vigorous push to the screen door with my back hand—bang—the signal for my mother to start a fire to cook breakfast on our wood-fired cook stove.

The stove had the name "Majestic" emblazoned in

large chrome letters on the oven door. The name
was incongruous, for did not fit in with its present
humble surroundings. It did however evoke in me
contemplation of a world filled with possibilities that
was waiting.

Running down the path toward the lake, I gained
momentum as my feet reached the dock, trying not to
trip on the areas where boards were missing. I dove
into the water, clearing the near-shore weeds that grew
in abundance close to shore.

The water felt cool, refreshing and delicious as it
slipped over and covered my slim body. I was pleased
I was becoming more successful each time in hurtling
my body over the slimy weeds into deeper water. My
body automatically went into a kick-crawl stroke as I
headed across the lake. This ritual of going for a swim
across the lake and touching Mr. Hautala's dock and
swimming back to our place before eating breakfast
went on all summer long, the first summer at our new
home. It was an activity that I thoroughly enjoyed.

My ability to swim across the lake by myself amazed
my mother, but she wasn't concerned that this was a
dangerous recreational activity for a ten-year-old boy.

In later years I read that during the famine in
Ireland, it was considered a blessing if a child would

accidentally perish while playing or passing his time in the nearby ocean waters.

I climbed out of the water onto our dock, panting, but with a feeling of exhilaration. Unknown to me then, that aerobic and vigorous exercise caused endorphins to enter my bloodstream, causing elation and an elevated feeling of well-being.

This delightful ritual of mine was also topped off with an exceptional breakfast. By the time I got back home, breakfast would be ready. Steaming strong coffee, fried fish left over from the catch the day before, and fried potatoes. Next, we went fishing for supper, and if we were lucky, food for the next day. We had our fishing lines wrapped around a rectangular piece of old discarded wood board, two lines, one for my mother and one for me.

One of the skills we learned in fishing for food was to use a lure instead of bait. Lures were economical to buy and replace. They were tough, lasted many fishing trips, and had the certainty of catching some Northern Pike.

Northern Pike was not as delectable as a Walleye Pike, but we liked it. Regardless the way we cooked a Northern Pike, whether it was fish soup with potatoes (kala moijakka) or pan fried with fried potatoes, it was delicious to a hungry person.

Once the boat was moving, by rolling the wood board and unraveling the line, the lure would be in the water, making its inviting red- and white-colored movement, as it hid its deadly triple hook. The amount of line that we unraveled would determine the lure's depth level, and also the intensity of human sounds reaching below the water's surface. Greater distance contributes to quietness and a more natural underwater ambience and better fishing.

The modern rods and reels were being used by those that could afford to buy them. They were efficient, and fun, but costly. And when one did not have the money, one learned to improvise. We used a scrap piece of discarded board and wrapped our lines around it. The short boards and bamboo poles were standard fishing gear, before rods and reels were invented. There was nothing to go wrong with them. The cost was minimal for the cheap line that went on the wood piece. The best part was that our boards with wrapped line and lures worked. We caught fish.

Our boat was an "old timer," given to us by a generous neighbor. The boat was scarred up from hard usage over the years. Its pine boards were starting to decompose because of age and improper storage. All of these factors contributed to a leaking boat and the chore of bailing the boat out with a rusty tin can every thirty minutes or so.

Rowing a boat for three or four hours every day was work. My hands developed calluses and my body became hard. As I dipped my oars into the water, I pushed with my legs and feet against the vacant seat in front of me, and at the same time pulled hard on the oars with my arms and back, causing the boat to move ahead with certainty. My mother sat on the stern seat, with both boards, with fishing lines in her hands and a prayer in her heart, that a fish would grab one or both of the daredevils.

Her prayers were answered, because we caught a lot of Northern Pike. It was always an exciting time, because they were noted for their lively resistance to being taken out of their native habitat. I would quit rowing, take the board without the fish, wrap the line up quickly to prevent the lure, from the boat's lack of motion, to drop down into the weeds, and the hooks to get snagged on the weeds or the bottom and possibly break a line and lose a costly twenty five-cent lure.

At home with fish to clean, mother got the wood stove going. Potatoes, onions and cleaned fresh fish were dropped into the frying pan—the ingredients for a gourmet meal, indeed! The daily activities were to be repeated over and over again throughout the summer. We had good times, a good life, and fun. That was life on Lawrence Lake. Those years were the best.

Chapter 15
Back to Bovey and Evil

Circumstances changed, my mother got employment in a hotel and so regrettably, we moved back to Bovey. I say regrettable because the thought of writing of my experiences while my mother was employed at the hotel brings on unhappy thoughts. Regrettably, this part of the story is sordid and difficult to write about.

The proprietors of the hotel where my mother was employed had a son, a man in his late thirties. He had a passion for pursuing young boys for sexual purposes. Later, it became known to me that the perversion of this man was known to most of the townspeople. However, in that time period, there was not the education, the openness, or newspaper or TV reports to protect and inform the public about sexual deviants living in communities. No one will ever know how many young boys were degraded and hurt by the deviant interests of this man.

Talk about this family was done in hushed voices, probably because of the family's wealth. They owned several hotels, a large road construction company, and had other business interests. They were the wealthiest people in Bovey and very likely, northern Minnesota. My mother and I were not privy to gossip or talk of any kind, especially of this family.

I learned more about this man later in my life, after my own experiences with him. His story was told to me in bits and overheard when others were having conversations about his behavior. When he was young, he had been sent to a Catholic priest school, but because of his sexual interests, he was requested to leave the school and prohibited from pursuing his interests in becoming a priest. He came back to Bovey.

Because of his interest and influence, it was arranged to have me keep my things and sleep in a separate building, also owned by this family, across the street from the hotel.

It was a large room with two beds. One bed was mine; the other bed was occupied by a man that appeared to be drunk or sleeping in a drunken state most of the time. Shortly after I moved into this room, I was awakened late at night by the sound of a key opening the door's lock. The squeaky sound of rusty hinges warned me that the door was slowly being opened. The occupant of the other bed was already noisily sleeping in a drunken state. I wondered who was entering the room.

The top of the door frame had a small rectangular window with a dual purpose. First of all, it allowed room ventilation and it let in some light, especially at night from the hallway lights.

Because of the dim lighting, I could see the profile of a huge man approaching my bed. Even in this subdued light I could see that the man looked like the hotel owner's son. He was bent over and beginning to kneel, with his hands groping. Even though I was fourteen years old, I was scared.

A multitude of things ran through my mind: back alley talk, including stories of perversion. I thought of my mother's employment. If I said anything to anyone in authority, my mother's employment would stop. If I told the police, who would believe me? He was a rich man's son; it would be his word against the word of a fatherless boy. We were a poverty stricken mother and son. Telling the authorities would give another reason, for those that are so inclined, to mock me with cutting barbs.

Wealth was a license to do wrong. I felt shame and guilt that has never left me, ever. My mother never knew or found out about how costly her job at the hotel had been. My mother continued working at the hotel for several more months. I decided that it was time to leave school and get a job.

Chapter 16
A Job in an Iron-Ore Mine

The world, the country, and the Iron Range were changing. Pearl Harbor occurred, and then in 1942, my personal life changed, for I quit school, two weeks into the ninth grade. The iron mines were booming, so I went to their employment office and applied for a job.

"How old are you?" I was asked by an authoritative voice, a voice that was so deep that it sounded as if it were coming from a deep well. With my knees shaking, and with my ever present inward qualms, at age fifteen I knew that if I told him that I was eighteen, there could be some doubt, questions, and possibly research into school records, so I mustered up all the courage and grit in self talk, stood upright and made myself as tall and old looking as I could, and looked him straight in the eye and in a loud clear voice, "I am twenty-three years old." The immediate response was, "Go take your physical tomorrow. You have a job."

I worked for the mining company eight months without a draft card. For my mother, the security of having a son with a steady job and income was comforting. I felt the thrill of earning a man's wages.

I was doing something constructive. I was achieving something. I was mastering a man's job, even though I had quit school at fifteen years of age. My regret over quitting school, guilt feelings, and a deepening self doubt, were forcibly pushed aside. Life continues regardless of how one feels, and as the old cliché goes, "you play the hand that you were dealt."

I was repeatedly asked for my draft card, but my response was evasive and deceptive. Then lying in bed one night, a thought came to me, perhaps from my subconscious, where it had been long incubating. If this job does not pan out, why not go to the West Coast? There were employment possibilities, and branches of the military were a last resort. They were waiting.

I could steal off quietly on my own, a few coins in my pocket. The thought frightened, yet exhilarated me. I continued to nurture this dream, fascinated by it. Then one day, I was informed that I had to produce a draft card or that I would be laid off. It was then I told them my correct age. I hoped that because of my industriousness and dependability I would be kept on as an employee, regardless of my age. But my work record did not have any value, and I was out of a job.

Chapter 17
Leaving Minnesota

My last paycheck was large, because in those days, the mining company policy was to hold back two weeks pay. So I gave my mother the money and kept thirty dollars. I told her that I was going to hitchhike to the West Coast. My mother was, understandably, upset. She already had two sons in the service—the U.S. Army and the U.S. Air Force. Now her youngest son, who had just turned sixteen, was leaving her. She consented, because by now, she was accustomed to life's vagaries, and from her old country perspective, a sixteen-year-old was mature.

I left home with the clothes on my back and as much as I could pack into my satchel—which was about the size of the kind of satchel that doctors used to carry—and thirty dollars. My plans were to go to Seattle, and to hitchhike night and day until I got there. I thought I would look for employment and if, for any reason, I was unable to get work, I would enlist either in the U.S. Marine Corps, the U.S. Navy or the U.S. Army Paratroopers.

Hitchhiking was good. I would get out of one car, and soon, I would be in another, moving constantly westward. Small Minnesota farms and lakes turned into larger farms and the rich soil of the Red River Valley. I saw cars, pickups and then more expensive cars. Soon, pungent odors emanated from the stock yards of West Fargo, then the plains of North Dakota—it was like watching a travelogue, and I was in it.

I felt free from responsibilities. I had lost my employment through no fault of my own. I knew my mother had enough money to take care of her needs for several months. Knowing this added to my spirit of adventure.

Hitchhiking was fun and problematic at the same time. Occasionally, my ride terminated before a town, before a crossroad, or in some out-of-the-way place. When that happened, I had to walk long distances in order to get to a more advantageous location for hitching rides.

Chapter 18
A Train West

In North Dakota, the highway went by a railroad depot. A lengthy passenger train, pulled by a large Malley Train Engine, had just pulled into the Bismarck railroad depot. Many people were at the station, servicemen, service women and other; Some were getting on the train, some were getting off the train. Groups of people were engaged in conversations, goodbyes, or just looking on.

The Malley Engine was like a prize fighter being attended to between rounds, for the workers scurried here and there, their back pockets bulging with rags, and with flashlights, tools and oil cans in their hands. And above everything else, on the engine and almost like a picture frame, was the engineer's window.

I saw the Malley locomotive engineer. It was a heady appellation. An authoritarian stance was an incidental, unwritten part of his job description. He was the person that was going to drive this steam belching beast down the railroad tracks towards that sinking sun in the west.

All the activity got my interest. I asked one of the railroad employees, where the train was going. "West

Coast, in fact to Seattle, Washington. It would take thirty to thirty-six hours."

I found myself formulating a plan. I started looking for an out of the way place to put on my overalls, top and bottom. With my new change of clothing, including a red handkerchief around my neck, I climbed a rusty, sooty ladder, just like I belonged to the train crew. I found an area, just large enough for me to sit down in, on the uppermost part of the engine without being seen by the engine crew or anyone else.

Soon, the big, impressive looking beast started to move. It had six large steam-driven wheels on each side, each wheel attached to a circular shaft of glistening finished steel. The shaft went in and out of a steam cylinder with each revolution of the wheel. Steam escaped with each stroke, fleetingly obscured the side of the engine.

A ruddy-faced engineer was at his station. One hand on the whistle cord, which he sounded numerous times for numerous reasons. It was a deep-throated, multi-toned whistle, a sound that generated one's immediate respect, and could be heard for miles. His other gloved hand was on the throttle. The engineer was clothed in a denim cap that matched his suspender overalls and jacket, a faded worn blue color because of usage. The large red handkerchief around his neck stood out in stark contrast and completed the color scheme.

It was an awesome sight indeed, a Malley R.R. Engine, pulling a string of passenger cars and a single red caboose following behind, racing through the prairie at seventy plus miles per hour. A throaty whistle sounded repeatedly a mile before a highway road crossing, followed by a nebulous cloud of steam then quickly dispersed into the atmosphere.

An awesome ride for the unpaying, ticketless passenger, that was drinking in the sights and sounds, experiencing a departure from the antiseptically clean, ninth grade classroom that I had been sitting in less than a year before.

With the train's momentum, a slow rocking movement developed, from side to side. This movement, combined with the clickety-clack sound of the wheels, as they run over tracks (before seamless tracks) was relaxing, and caused me to fall asleep. The train rolled on monotonously through the night. The train's high speed caused a whirlwind of smoke, cinders and coal dust. The train's whistle was loud and next to where I was sitting. I began to feel regret that I had got on the train. Every moment that I can bear some discomfort is getting me closer to

Seattle, so what is a little pain, I thought?

Eventually, I climbed down off the engine, and sat down on the step of the first passenger car. It was quieter, cleaner and more enjoyable. As I was sitting there, apparently a black dining car waiter had seen me. He stepped down and handed me a ham sandwich, wrapped in a napkin, and with a wide smile and a "good luck brother," he departed. I have never forgotten the incident, and over the years, I have returned similar favors to others that were in need. This practice will never leave me.

Soon I heard an angry voice swearing at me. I turned and looked, it was a conductor, dressed in black, finely creased trousers, shined, high-top black shoes and a solid, quality black, official looking cap, with silver band and metal work, with the unmistakable engraving that spelled out CONDUCTOR.

"What the hell are you doing here?"

"Going out West," I replied.

"What are you doing, running away from the army?"

"No, I'm not old enough," I answered. "Do you want to see my birth certificate?"

"No, I don't want to see your birth certificate. I want to see your ticket. We are coming to a water stop in twenty minutes, a place called Custer, Montana. You get off there. If you don't, and I see you on here again, I will throw you off," he replied with coldness and anger, in his voice and face. When the train slowed down, I jumped off with my satchel. I did not want to face the conductor again.

Chapter 19
Hitchhiking Again

I walked down the dark highway with my satchel, and after a while, a distant red light came into view. It turned out to be an all night combination gas station and restaurant. I went into their washroom and stripped to my waist, and washed and washed. I was filthy. It took fifteen minutes of scrubbing, and sheets of paper toweling, and I was presentable.

After a hamburger, coffee, and a conversation with a long distance truck driver, I was headed westward, again. The primary reason for picking up a hitchhiker is conversation. In a half an hour, we would be friends. In an hour and a half, we would be brothers. Before the ride was over, I would know the driver's life history, what was wrong with his ex-wife, the best truck stop for food on U.S. 2, and the best place to pick up women in Waco, Texas.

Eventually, I arrived at Columbus, Montana. For some reason, prospects for hitching a ride diminished. Possibly the reason was that Columbus was at the base of the Rocky Mountain Range, and going westward was a tedious upward climb, a drive that required more attention to driving and less time talking.

Chapter 20
Back on the Rails

After a while, a young man that I had seen at a distance glancing in my direction walked up and struck up a conversation. The young man, Elmer, told me that he was interested in traveling to Spokane, Washington. He commented that a logical way to get out of town was the Great Northern Railroad. He went home, packed up his pack, bid his mother goodbye, and the two of us climbed into a railroad gondola car, which is designed with short sides and no top, making it easier to load with bulky cargo. Soon, a big Malley had us moving westward.

Building a railroad over any mountain range is obviously a challenging task. Going through a mountain, or circling the mountain, the valleys and surrounding terrain was visually taking place as the train advanced westward. The curves were severe. We would catch up to the tail end of our train with its red caboose going in the opposite direction, a 180 degree difference in course direction. Soon, another Malley Engine joined our train group and was coupled behind the caboose, so that we had one Malley pulling the chain of several hundred cars and another Malley pushing, the snake like formation of railroad cars and engines.

When the train went through a mountain tunnel, with Elmer and me sitting in our gondola car, we discovered a buildup of darkness, smoke, and heat. The longer the tunnel, the more intense was the smoke and heat and the more uncomfortable our ride became. We could not get off the moving train, so in silent thought, I wondered if we would survive the ride or if our young lives would be snuffed out in suffocation on a stolen ride in a railroad gondola. We could not see, or talk to one another in the hot, smoky, darkness, so I did not know what Elmer was doing, or how he was faring.

In one exceptionally long tunnel, in desperation, I whipped out my shirt tail, and wrapped it around my head, and lay on the floor of the car, praying. The movement of the train was laborious and slow. Laying in the darkness, on the floor of that railroad gondola in hot, concentrated smoke was pushing my anxiety level. Self-talk, and knowing Elmer was having the same experience, gave me some assurance that we would survive. Eventually, the darkness turned to light, and two young boys, grateful to still be living got off the train at the first stop.

Chapter 21
Spokane

Eventually, we arrived at Spokane, Washington. We went to The Y.M.C.A. and were accommodated with bunks, lockers, hot showers and a place to wash our clothes—all at a reasonable cost. It was a godsend, indeed.

Across the street from The Y.M.C.A. was a huge hotel, the Davenport. It covered an entire city block It encompassed numerous businesses besides hotel rooms. The Davenport reeked of quality and class. Walking by it brought on feelings of grandeur and respect. The word was out that young men could find employment as busboys in a part of the hotel that had the name "Italian Gardens," for small wages and food.

Elmer and I were hired as busboys. We were fitted out with white coats, sport coat length. The busboy captain had us line up and he walked and checked out our hands, finger nails, clothes and shoes. Then he gave us basic instructions: clear the tables as the dining guests left, put on clean tablecloths, set the tables with eating utensils, and napkins, walk around with a cart and silver water pitcher looking for water glasses that needed filling—and how to do all of these tasks with an air of efficiency and professionalism.

The waiters wore tuxedos and the waitresses wore skirts and blouses that had a distinct European flavor. A bandstand seated at least a dozen musicians. They played soothing, beautiful music that enhanced the opulence of Italian Gardens. The waiters and the waitresses tipped the busboys. The wages, even though they were small, combined with the tips, added up. I felt that I should be moving on and I now had enough money to ride on public transportation, so I took a bus to Seattle.

Chapter 22
Seattle and the Merchant Marines

Seattle had a distinct, salty, primordial flavor. The odor of the ocean—I liked it then, I still do. It brought on visions of the romance of travel and the oceans of the world that seemed to be my destiny. It was an exciting time. Brought up in the country and small villages, and now I was in the metropolis of Seattle, teeming with people, service men, whose uniforms were readily discernible.

Then it happened. A group of uniformed men came into view. They wore uniforms that I had not seen before and could not identify. When we were about to pass each other, going in opposite directions, I asked them what branch of the service did their uniforms represent? "U.S. Merchant Marine, and they need men," one of them replied. I quickly asked directions to the merchant marine recruiting office.

The walk to the recruiting office turned out to be an adventure. First of all, it was not like a visit to a Sunday school class. Located on the waterfront, I went down First Street, then Yesler Way. The streets had saloons, tattoo parlors and boarded up burlesque halls, places that filled a need during the Klondike gold rush days. There were people that were sober and others in various stages of intoxication. Sailors, stevedores, racy looking women with inviting smiles and other people looking for adventure.

On one corner there was a Salvation Army brass band that played loud, rousing, come hither music, complete with a convincing looking preacher who took over after the music, using strong words to reach out to those on the streets where the lonely walked and were hungry for human contact and words that assured them that life was worth living.

The office quickly gave me an application. At the bottom of the page was a place where parental consent was requested. I told the office person that I would be back shortly. I could feel that they were not overly concerned about the accuracy of the information requested on the application, which made deception an easy option. There was a war going on and they needed men to man their ships and one way or another, they were going to get them.

I stood on the cracked sidewalk, contemplating what would be the best way to get my mother's signature on that application. I knew my mother would readily give her consent, but she was in Minnesota. I could either sign my mother's name in the designated space or I could find another way. I did not want to screw up. I wanted this signature to be authentic and believable.

The thought of becoming a merchant marine sailor suddenly became the most important issue in my sixteen years of life.

I sauntered into a nearby smoke-filled waterfront bar full of sailors, longshoremen and other civilians. The jukebox, which emanated flowing colors, bubbles and eye catching action, had the volume turned up so that the heart-wrenching songs about unrequited love spilled out into the street. I picked out a middle-aged waitress who had just snuffed out a cigarette butt and was about to swing back into her work.

I explained my intent to become a sailor and that my mother was in Minnesota. I needed a signature, would she help me out? "Sure, sonny, where would you want me to sign?" she replied, while exhaling the remains of that last drag. Her loud voice and brassy manner got the attention of the bar's occupants, customers and employees alike. A human interest story was taking place right before their eyes.

I brought the application into the Merchant Marine recruiting office. The office person explained to me that a ten day seaman training class was about to begin. The training would take place on an old wooden ship named The U.S.A.T. Sierra. The ship was tied up to a buoy in Puget Sound. After a physical, I was transported to The Sierra in a motorized lifeboat.

I chose training in the deck department because I
wanted to be working outside the ship, rather than
the engine room or the galley department. We
were civilian seamen, but we were allowed to wear
modified navy uniforms. The ten days of training
was intense. We studied, memorized and recited
the compass rose by heart. We learned how to make
an eye splice, a long splice, and a short splice. We
learned to tie a bowline, a sheepshank, half hitches
and other knots. We learned the parts of a ship, the
color and designated places for the ship's running
lights. We learned how to steer a ship by using
a magnetic compass. And we learned to lower a
lifeboat as a team in a simulated emergency situation.

After we lowered a life boat, we were cast loose from
the Sierra. We rigged up what they called a "jury rig,"
an emergency sail rig. We sailed around Puget Sound
while an instructor continuously lectured to us. He
had rolled up his sleeves, revealing hairy arms and
aged tattoos. He was an old salt, and he looked the
part. He constantly referred to past experiences that
he had acquired in a lifetime of sailing. Even though
it was apparent, he still reminded us that these
lessons were verbal, not out of a textbook, and he
repeatedly exclaimed, "You'd better listen, for some
day your life may depend on it."

We opened up the emergency tinned life boat rations, canned pemmican. Pemmican was concentrated mixture of vegetable oil, raisins, nuts and other now forgotten ingredients. It was said that teaspoon of pemmican would sustain a person for several days.

After ten days, on graduation day, we were assigned to a building called the Cadre to wait for an assignment aboard a ship. We, the trainees in the deck department, now had a rank. We were called "Ordinary Seamen," the bottom rung in the deck department. We were well on the way to becoming real sailors on an ocean-going ship.

Chapter 23
Becoming a Seaman

After two days in the Cadre, I was assigned to the M.G. Zalinski, an old ship that had been built around 1900. Three thousand ton, it had four holds. The top parts of the holds were refrigerated, designed to keep perishable cargo. The bottom parts of the holds were designed to hold general cargo. We also carried deck cargo, anything from lumber to military equipment. The Zalinski was now underway, headed for sea.

There were three sea watches in a 24-hour day: the 12 to 4, the 4 to 8, and the 8 to 12 watches, three seamen to a watch. Two held the rank Able Body Seaman, which means they were experienced seaman that had passed a U.S. Coast Guard examination and then were issued an Able Seaman's and Life Boat Certificate. There was one Ordinary Seaman. All three of us spent one hour and twenty minutes on the steering wheel, an hour and twenty minutes on look out, and one hour and twenty minutes on standby. This totaled four hours, comprising a sea-watch.

Distant lights were pointed out as Port Angelas. Countless seagulls, flying over the stern of the Zalinski made excited sounds while surveying the dumping of the ship's garbage on the stern. The brisk, briny smelling wind increased, whistling through the rigging. The waves increased in size, affecting the motion of the ship. The ship's brass bell gonged every half hour, letting those that were in their bunks or out on deck know the time of the day. I was learning to swing my body up and into my top bunk. The sight of a six-inch cannon on our stern and bow and the twenty millimeter anti-aircraft guns next to the wheelhouse was disconcerting. This was not a battleship, only an American freighter in time of war. Everything contrasted sharply with the world that I had left behind. The Zalinski would be an awesome sight to any landlubber, especially to a sixteen-year-old who had been sitting in a ninth grade classroom less than a year ago.

The North Pacific ocean greeted the Zalinski and crew with mountainous valleys of briny sea water that fall day in 1943. And to me on my first voyage, it seemed that it would also be the last one. The thought crossed my mind that the ocean would surely sink our ship and send us to a watery grave. Our small ship would repeatedly and valiantly climb those valleys of water until the ship was vertical like a skyscraper, and then come crashing down, causing mountains of water to wash over the bow and bury it and the hatches, and then it would continue its momentum, crashing and expending its energy against the house of the ship, seeking that part of the

Leaning on the capston

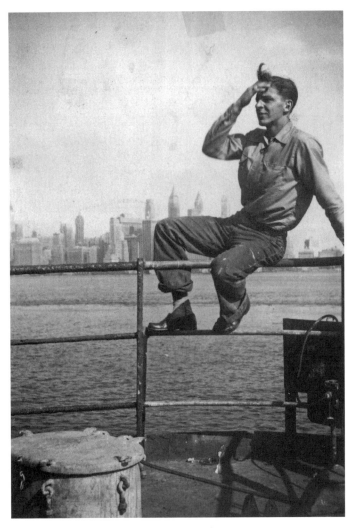

Ahoy Sailor

Zalinski that would be vulnerable and succumb to its energy.

This had been a hectic day, for we found ourselves in hurricane force winds that were gusting up to one hundred and fifty miles per hour, shrieking in the highest treble and as if by command snarling in the lowest base. We had the starboard life boat torn off. We lost our deck cargo of lumber during the day, and the weather was worsening." I didn't think this sailing business was going to be this bad," another first trip sailor uttered to me with compressed lips. "Me neither," was my terse reply.

I had finished my sea watch (8-12) and was looking forward to turning in for the night. The ambience of our living quarters (focsul) went unseen in the darkness. This included the odor from the nearby rope locker, oilskins drying out in the lockers, toilet and urinal for twelve men living and sleeping in close proximity. The lights-out policy was a courtesy agreed upon because of consideration for those seamen that were off watch trying to sleep. In the darkness, as I was settling into my bunk (I had the highest one up which is reserved for ordinary seamen) when the steel entrance door opened and forcibly slammed shut and the lights came on.

It was the bosun. A fifty-plus-year-old man with

probably more than half those years in sailing time and seamanship experience. He was the supervisory sailor responsible for seeing that the Captain's and the deck officers' orders were carried out. Glancing neither to the left nor to the right, he strode indomitably to the center of the room, and in a clear voice, gruff with age and resonant with authority, announced," All hands on deck, get your oilskins on, and meet in the mess hall. The tarp on number two hatch was damaged by the deck cargo that we lost. The ship is taking in more water than the pumps can handle. We have to replace the tarp immediately."

The mess hall was located midship, and the focsul (deck crew quarters) were on the stern of the ship. The wind was gusting, and the decks were awash. On the short walk to the mess hall, we got an indication of the seriousness of the task that we faced. Stepping through the steel bulkhead door to the mess hall, our rubber boots, oilskins and southwesterns (seaman's weather caps) drenched and dripping on the mess hall deck, we could see the bosun and the rest of the crew were waiting and ready.

The bosun rose and raised himself on his tiptoes and fairly crushed us with his glance, as was his intention, "You guys listen, if you want to live a little longer. You have never been in a situation as serious as this. Believe me, because I know what I am talking about. If you should get washed overboard, the ship will never turn around to look for you because we could sink the ship in this kind of sea if we tried. You should also know that we can't use lights, because this kind of weather does not affect submarines and their work."

"So again, I say listen. When we get to the hatch, you position yourselves so that there are an equal number of men on all four sides. You will be able to feel it in your legs when the ship is ascending or descending. When the downward descent is through, the bow of the ship will be buried deeply under the waves and that means the upward ascent is about to begin. Hang on tightly immediately, because there will be an unseen wall of water coming at you in the darkness. Unless you are hanging on tightly, you will be washed away. So, grab hold of the hatch, lower your head and crouch, so as to make a smaller profile, then the water can get by you easier. The weight of the water that will hit you will push you down to your knees. When the flow of water lets up and you can feel the ship starting to rise, then we will work. By that time, you eyes will have acclimated themselves to the darkness."

"We will set the replacement tarp on the most forward part of the hatch, towards the bow of the ship, rolling the tarp towards the stern, using the ship's momentum and the wind's direction to our advantage. Now let's go!"

We stumbled out of the seeming safety of the mess hall into the shrieking, watery darkness. We grabbed onto whatever our hands came onto as we made our way forward to number two hatch to keep it from being blown or washed overboard, as the water rushed between our legs and body.

The hurricane-force winds and gusts blew through the rigging of the masts and lashed-down booms and entered into cavities on the ship's surface, howling and screaming. The Zalinski rose and descended, rolling, while wildly moving water poured over the deck and around our bodies. One moment, the sea water was as high as your crotch and belt line, the next moment the steel deck on which you were standing was bare.

As we worked and moved around number two hatch, wordlessly communicating with each other, the work of replacing a hatch cover was being accomplished. We rolled the replacement tarp over the hatch, removed the steel flat bar, clamped off the old tarp and tucked the replacement tarp in place, reinstalling the steel flat bar. All of this was being done while the ship performed its gyrations, climbing a valley of water until it was almost vertical and then pitching downward, the bow burying itself under the surface of the sea. The propeller would be out of the water at this time, momentarily racing wildly, until the sea rushed in and filled the void in the propeller area and then the propeller grabbed hold of the sea, creating and adding a different sound to the existing medley of sounds and vibrations.

Finally, the bosun made a motion with his hand, indicating that this seemingly impossible task was finished. The seamen and I made our way to the steel bulkhead door. I felt emotions of satisfaction and a gratitude to the deity. I felt thankful for the presence of the bosun, for his competency and leadership skills. I was also cognizant of the positive way that we all worked together and the unseen forces that were with us that night as we learned to become merchant mariners, working to replace a damaged tarp on the number two hatch of a sinking ship, the M.G. Zalinski.

The mess hall was filled with seamen and their wet oilskins, holding cups of fresh strong coffee. Cigarette smoke spilled out into the passage ways and the sound of relaxed, animated voices talking about the dangers of the job just finished, and the shore leave that would be coming up in a week or so. There were silent and vocal thoughts about girls and the enjoyment there would be in sipping whiskey late into the night.

We stopped at Anchorage with supplies for the U.S. Army, and then Ketchikan, Petersburg and Pelican Inlet and loaded our refrigerated holds with boxes of fish and onto Seattle. The ensuing voyages to Alaska were similar with the exception of the North Pacific Ocean storm that we encountered on the first voyage. That storm was the worst that I experienced in my four years of sailing on the oceans of the world, including the North Atlantic during the winter months.

Chapter 24
A Wheelsman

I got off the Zalinski in January 1944. I was then assigned to The U.S.A.T. Restorer as a wheelsman. A wheelsman was called by the name of Quartermaster. His job was to steer the ship. He stood sea watches of four hours on and eight hours off, like the other sailors. He was given a 20 minute coffee break during his four hour watch. A wheelsman was more responsible and therefore it was a better job than an Able Seaman. Usually, only those who were considering making the merchant marine a career, and pursuing a lifetime job as a deck officer and eventually captain took the wheelsman's job.

The Restorer was a telegraph cable layer that was owned by Canada. It had been leased to the American government during W.W.II. The ship was designed to lay telegraph cable on the ocean floor. The Quartermasters were assigned two to a cabin. It was a vastly improved accommodation, in fact luxurious, compared to the focsul of the Zalinski. We proceeded to an area close to Attu, called Shemija, part of the Aleutian Island chain. Several of the islands, Kiska and Attu had been recently evacuated by the Japanese when attacked by American forces. We were accompanied by two destroyers. We started laying our cable at a specific latitude and longitude located between Japan and Shemija. We were going in the direction of Kodiak Island and the U.S.A.

The two destroyers cruised back and forth while we were doing our work, giving all of us the realization of the military importance that was being attached to our work. A Japanese surveillance plane flew over one day, a blazing rising sun on each side of the plane. It stayed just long enough for a flight of fighter planes from the American airfield at Attu to make their appearance, with guns blazing hot in pursuit of the single plane headed for Japan. We did not hear of the outcome.

We exhausted our supply of cable on our four month cruise and arrived back in Seattle in April 1944. April 11, my seventeenth birthday, was spent at sea. A great age, but also an age when one easily assimilates or rejects into one's own character the good or the bad values of others. I now felt older and I knew that I was constantly growing in skills, and again, very likely, whether good or bad, the speech and character, of a sea-going man.

I had three weeks to get to another assignment, which was a sea-going tugboat in the port of New York City. I stayed in Seattle just long enough for shore leave with my shipmates of four months—a celebration indeed, along with our final good-byes. And oh yes, a tattoo, the mark of a sailor, completed the picture. Skoal, shipmates. Goodbye, Seattle and the Pacific Ocean.

Chapter 25
On Leave

Minnesota and home. Regardless of past experiences and memories, some bad, some good, it was good to be back to Minnesota and mother. It so happened that my older brother Oscar was also home on leave from the U.S. Air force. Oscar was a sergeant in rank and had trained in multiple skills as crewman on various types of airplanes. So for over a week, we talked, visited, and ate mother's fried chicken.

Evenings, we frequented bars where strong drink and warmly smiling girls were at hand. I had been introduced to strong drink at an early age, first by family members, their friends and my friends, and with many of the people who lived on northern Minnesota's Iron Range. It was a place where taverns and saloons outnumbered all of the other businesses combined.

The Merchant Marine allowed for a continuation of this type of behavior and pastime. I did not need any further training. So, for my brother Oscar and me, to be on leave at the same time, was not a planned or fortuitous event. With the first drink, we were both happy and smiling, talking about past remembrances and the good times. By the second and third drink, talk was about the present as well as possible future years. The atmosphere became tense and the fourth drink led to chilly silence or flaming arguments. Soon, we only spoke to each other in a threatening way. Then, it had to come: a walk outside, blows were exchanged, and after a few bruises and scrapes, it ended in a grudging handshake.

This type of behavior was accepted and expected. One might say a "running with the bulls" approach to life seemed to be deeply encoded in the Antilla DNA. I have spent much of my life trying to undo this negativism. I didn't want to be remembered as the sixteen-year-old-boy who left home in 1943— rather, I wanted to be regarded as the individual I had become.

The days went by quickly, and soon we were again on our way. We bid our goodbyes in Chicago, and went our separate ways. Oscar went to an Air Force base in south-central U.S., and I went to New York City where a brand new sea-going tugboat was waiting to crew up and sail over to Europe and be a part of the Allied invasion of France. It dawned on me that history was being made, and I was a part of it. My sixteen months in Europe were filled with adventure, a few close ones, and survival, thanks to God.

Chapter 26
Friendship

I found friendship in shipmates, friendships that I had not experienced at home or elsewhere. We lived together; at times, we were on the same watch, therefore worked together; had our meals together, went ashore, imbibed in strong drink, looked for girls, got into fights, dodged torpedoes and bombs. They were a great bunch of guys to sail with. Now most of them have passed on. They were brothers indeed. The memories remain.

My two sea-bags and I, a small-town Minnesota boy, arrived in Grand Central Station, New York on a cold, rainy, overcast April day in 1944. How does one describe my culture shock? Here was a place, I thought, that people watchers must love: masses of people of different genetic origins, unabashedly speaking a variety of languages. I sensed a hurriedness, short, efficient, unfriendly answers, (bordering on rudeness) confidence, sophistication, and both rejection and acceptance.

My ship was in the Brooklyn Navy Yard. I had my first experience riding a subway and using transfers. Eventually I got to Brooklyn and the U.S.A.T. (Water Division) office. I received orders to report on a new seagoing tug boat L.T. 532, with the rank of Able Seaman. In brief, Able Seamen were called ABs. This rank usually required four years sea time. But in times of war, old rules were discarded, and young aspiring sailors learn quickly. No matter how demeaning the task, no matter how it broke the spirit, one had to do it, and most important, be able to do it.

Our ship (tug) was designed for crossing oceans in any kind of weather. Even though a seagoing tug boat is short in length compared to other ships, it was constructed in such a way that most of the ship was underneath the water line and therefore more stable, making it capable of surviving in any kind of ocean weather. The tug was also equipped with a massive engine, enabling it to tow barges, cranes, and disabled ships at sufficient speeds.

We had a crew of approximately fifty seamen, which also included ten U.S. Navy sailors. They were called the armed guard and their duties were to man and operate the guns. The entire crew was of all ages, from seventeen to seventy. At seventeen, I was the youngest.

Because of the small size of the ship and the numerous members of the crew, living quarters were cramped. The bunks were layered, one on top of the other, with about two feet of space between each bunk. The row went up about four bunks high. I was given the top bunk. Therefore it was a physical as well as an acrobatic achievement to get into my bunk: I would climb up and step on the edge of three lower bunks, grasp a steel post, swing my body from a vertical position to a horizontal one, and finally swing into my bunk. While in my bunk, I read well-used magazines or books from the ship's library (a cardboard box) until sleep came, and when I awoke, it was time to perform these same gymnastics to climb out of my bunk.

The individual bunks were about two inches from the ship's hull. On one side of the steel hull were the freezing cold waters of the North Atlantic. On the other side of the steel hull was the warm living quarters of the crew. The result: condensation. One could see rivulets of water dripping down the hull to the main deck and accumulating into pools of water, water that would spread out onto that part of the deck that was dry. This went on until someone came up with a solution to collect the water. We spread out shower towels in the problem areas, and then wrung them out periodically. A solution and an improvement.

A new ship, a new crew, and a marked change for all of us, more for some than others. The stench of fifty sweating seamen combined with the odor of diesel oil from the nearby engine compartment, the smell of food and moldy bread, and the offensive odors that emanated from the galley and the two tiny washrooms. As the ship rocked and lurched, we contemplated the discomforts of the seaman's life, but we never openly talked about it. Complaining would be a sign of weakness. After all, we were now a part of the fabled merchant marine, where stoicism prevailed.

Chapter 27
England

The word was out: our destination was England. A driving rain pelted the sailors in our oilskin rain gear as we worked to secure deck cargo, hatches, tarps and other items for the long voyage across the Atlantic. Loose deck cargo is extremely dangerous. On the oceans, there is always a possibility of a storm coming up quickly. Ships have been damaged and sunk because of unsecured or improperly secured items on deck or in the holds.

Soon our ships were positioned, hundreds of them, in convoy formation, and we were moving. The ships all had a uniform color, battleship gray. The gray color was another safety measure, because it was the color least detectable by roving submarine periscopes. Our convoy consisted of ships from many countries, the U.S.A., England, Norway, Greece and other countries.

Many of the Greek ships as well as ships from other countries were of vintage years. Old ships had an effect on the safety factor of the convoy, because the speed of the whole convoy was determined by the fastest speed of the slowest ship. A slow-moving convoy gave submarines an advantage in sending their torpedoes with greater accuracy. A good example of how important a ship's speed in time of war is the H.M.S. Queen Mary. Her speed was so fast, that she didn't have to travel with other ships or have a battleship escort. She traveled at her maximum speed, using a zig-zag course across the Atlantic from the U.S.A. to England. She made countless voyages across the Atlantic carrying American and Canadian military personal and survived WW II. She is a tourist attraction in California, a reminder of WW II.

An interesting aspect of Greek ships, and perhaps ships of other countries was their lack of food storage facilities, such as freezer rooms. So, in order to have enough food for an extended voyage, they carried animals such as pigs, sheep, and cattle on their main deck, then butchered and had fresh meat whenever their food supply needed replenishing.

The movement of the deck under your feet, the sound of the ship's bell, denoting the time of the watch, and the sight of a sea of swaying ship's masts, brought one's thoughts back to the present. The sound of distant depth charges brought on the realization that this was no ordinary voyage. The German submarine fleet had been the king of the seas for early part of the war. But now, the tide had turned. The allied escort ships, destroyers, cruisers, equipped with their up to date sub-killing technology, had made the difference.

The enemy was still out there, but their numbers and fascistic philosophy had been diminished and damaged.

The good weather ended and gale force winds developed, soon lashing the waves to tremendous heights. Under a menacing sky, thick with dark clouds, waves developed into mountainous size, toying with our small boat, tossing her wildly and keeping the wings of the bridge half filled with water. The LT 532 worked frantically to maintain her designated position in the convoy. We charged forward, spreading foam and spray. The wind howled and the waves thundered.

Chapter 28
Under Fire

Suddenly, there was a blast—a nearby ship caught one or several torpedoes. The area below the second hatch was blazing with flame, a fireball, then loud detonations. What we could see of the ship indicated that she was going down fast.

A huge fountain rose over the dying vessel. A second explosion, then a third. Chunks of steel were being hurtled in all directions. The stern of the 15,000 ton freighter broke off. The bow and the stern were burning furiously, illuminating nearby ships and the area. Collisions were being avoided with other ships, with difficulty and hard rudder maneuvers. Exploding cargo and flares turn the dark night into a bright inferno. I have wondered then and for years afterward, what about the men? Lowering lifeboats would have been very difficult as well as impossible because of the swiftness as well as the effectiveness of the torpedoes damage.

The ships usually went down fast. Submarines were the obvious danger for escort vessels to slow or stop their vessels to pick up anyone. When we went through our brief training less than a year ago, we were told that in case we had to jump off the ship into the water, we should lay on our backs, because our back muscles would more easily absorb the impact of depth charges.

Then, in the midst of this activity, an escort vessel, a destroyer, came out of the darkness, her bow rising knife-like, moved towards us. She was so close that we could see her marking numbers. Our boat turned to the starboard just in time to avoid a ramming. Because of this, we lost sight of the dying vessel, and the occasion to witness her demise.

Chapter 29
Hurricane

It is almost four a.m. and my four to eight watch takes over. I step into the wheelhouse. It is located at the highest part of the ship. I step up to the place where the wheelsman being relieved is standing. He is aware of my presence. He speaks softly to me, "Steering 94 degrees," and takes his hands off the brass steering wheel. I then grasp the wheel, and at the same time repeat, "Steering 94 degrees," and look at the small patch of light, that gives the direction in degrees, and is called a gyro compass. Nearby and alongside the gyro compass is a large, aged-looking, magnetic compass, that is only used in case of an emergency, an emergency that has stopped the gyro compass.

The LT 532 climbed the peaks of the waves with great effort. When we were at the tops of these waves, we were surrounded by the mountainous range of ocean water, littered with ships all heading in the same direction and facing the same seas, battling for survival, not from the submarines, but from the ocean. When one looked downward there were valleys of salty, briny water hundreds of feet below us.

The boat tumbled down into the bottoms of those valleys, burying herself in a foaming whirlpool, I was grateful for the buoyant, cork-like qualities the LT 532 was exhibiting Looking upward was like looking up at a skyscraper, at the tops of the waves, hundreds of feet above us. Momentarily, the waves were blending together, creating a curtain like shield that blotted out the sky, then starting its downward journey, obeying the laws of nature, weighing tons, the ocean was looking for a vulnerable place to disperse its killing energy—whether it would be a weakened bulk head, defective welding, a faulty porthole or worn parts of the ship that had been functioning well under sunny skies and peaceful oceans. Hurricane-force winds and the North Atlantic Ocean is another matter. Our propeller would come out of the water momentarily, spin wildly, until the water surges back with a rush, causing a momentary vibration as the prop catches hold.

The hurricane was steadily worsening, a nearby destroyer escort, was having problems and fighting for survival. They were affectionately called "cans" by sailors, and had a reputation for rolling in swells, rolling to the extent that they would take in water through their smoke stacks. Ship-handling skills and engine room pumps usually saved the day. A cargo ship with a damaged bridge swayed helplessly.

Other vessels with their propellers and most of their rudders in and out of the sea rode the tops of the cliff-like waves.

Gigantic walls of water mercilessly pounded against their hulls and superstructures, pushing the ship's rivet and weld construction to its limits. Everywhere, there were ships in distress. Battered lifeboats hanging crookedly from their davits, pinched smoke stacks, ripped loading hatches, deck cargo torn loose from their lashings and pushed by screaming waves and sea water over gunwales and into the sea. Breaker after breaker smashed rudders and probably bent shafts in the process. The ones that went down had no need for torpedoes, for torpedoes released in this savage sea, would never have reached their target.

Shipboard routine went on as usual. The mess boys took bed sheets and watered them down, to keep the dishes, pots and bowls of food from sliding onto the deck off the long dining table. Very little sea sickness was evident, probably because most of us were seasoned sailors and took the shuddering, listing, pitching movement with stoicism. The bow of the ship had a fifteen to twenty degree swing, so the wheelsman compensated by having equal degrees on each side of the given course that he was steering the ship by.

The sensation I had lying in my bunk while the ship was moving over the mountain-like waves was unique. The ship would be almost vertical going upward over a wave, then it would be almost vertical going downward over a wave. When the ship was moving upward, I sunk heavily into my bunk, stretching the canvas supporting my body to its limits, making me feel like I had doubled my weight, and a few moments later, the ship would start its downward trip, dropping again a great distance, making me feel light as a feather that had been cast out the window of an upper story apartment. These pleasant sensations brought on a deep sleep.

Chapter 30
Scotland

Land ahoy! The coast of Scotland came into view. Our ship put in to a little village, with the ancient name of Roseneath. A village that in peacetime was an idyllic coastal village, with old homes, on cobblestone streets, colorful, ivy-covered, ancient business buildings housing wares and essentials for everyday living. Then we saw the old piers, an occasional old man grasping a fishing pole in one hand, and a gnarled, old pipe in the other, with his legs dangling over the edge of the pier, fishing for eel. Because Great Britain was an Island, surrounded by the sea, he was probably a former seaman, who had been caught up in the rush of years, victimized by his inabilities as he grew older. His thoughts were the early years, and catching food for the supper table.

The piers were used by fishing boats of various sizes, and an occasional freighter, with supplies for the people of Roseneath and nearby cities and villages.

Now a transformation had taken place. The time: April 1944. Roseneath had become a closely guarded American submarine base. The piers were now occupied by ships of war. Destroyers, cruisers, minesweepers, other vessels, painted battleship gray with a aggressive appearance and ordinary freighters, that had become heavily armed freighters, with cannons on the bow and stern, with smaller anti-aircraft guns midships.

The piers were now occupied by sailors in various stages of sobriety and drunkenness, on their way back to their ships, or heading for shore leave, plying the streets of Roseneath in search of earthy forms of recreation. A single uniform is attractive, interesting, indicating a disciplined way of life. A bunch of uniforms multiplies the visual effect of youth, vigor, action—all summed up in the cliché, "prime of life." Our presence did not go unnoticed, as girls with romantic interests of their own became a part of the scene.

We were told our ship would be at Roseneath several days. Those that wanted to travel to Glasgow seventy miles away would be given passes and the liberty to go there. The word was out—shore leave would be better in Glasgow, because it was a populated city and there were not as many servicemen there. A ride on an interesting looking double decker bus further enhanced the trip.

Practically, the whole crew decided to go and almost filled up our large double decker bus, much to the displeasure of the local, older citizens, who preferred a more sedate, quiet and restful ride to the large city. Now what will happen with a bunch of Yanks aboard? Riding on the second floor of the bus was similar to being on a small ship. Any change in the road—hills, dips, and curves—were further accentuated in the swaying movement of the upper part of the bus. Of course, this brought out the kid in me that had never left.

Glasgow was interesting. Anything one wanted was available. Saloons, called pubs in the British Isles, were smoky and crowded, serving gin and ale of different sorts. Warm ale seemed to be the favorite, because it was the least expensive, only a six pence or a dime for a pint. The ale had various names: "mild," "bitter," and "nut brown." We heard "Limeys" order "half and half," half mild and half bitter ale. One soon caught on to the money exchange. Instead of the American, penny, nickel, quarter, and half dollar, they had the hae-penny, penny, thratenie bit, thra-pence, six-pence schilling, half crown, ten shilling note, pound, and five pound note.

A five pound note was worth twenty dollars. The different economies in the U.S.A. and Great Britain were a source of chagrin between the two countries. An example: the wages of the lowest ranked American serviceman was fifty dollars a month, equal to or more than the wages of the English workman. A pint of ale was six pence (a dime). The average English workman would come in a pub and nurse a pint for hours, amidst a lot of visiting, conversation and throwing darts.

The American G.I. or sailor would come in and toss down a pint in a few minutes. After a few more pints in quick succession, the inhibitions were gone, and the conversation acquired a barracks or focsul-like flavor. All women, attached or otherwise began to look warm and inviting.

That feeling that intoxication brings on returns, caused one to behave like he was back in The U.S.A. again, in a local bar, tossing drinks down with the objective of getting smashed. Money, he had lots of it—receiving fifty dollars a month, he could feel and live like a rich man. Hence, ill feelings came, causing disagreements, fights and stereotyping all the Yanks with clichés such as "overfed, overpaid, oversexed, and over here."

The underlying, trivial hostility eventually evolved into cohesiveness, mutual drinking bouts, and further invitations to homes, friendships, romances and marriages. The Americans called the Brits "Limeys." The English called America "The Colony," and the American servicemen, "The Yanks." All with a smile and a pat on the back.

The ride back to Roseneath had interesting things
to look at; faces, people, villages, countryside, a land
that had been subdued. The human element, and
its inherent tendency and hunger for a better life
contribute to stories and sagas where ever one travels.

Chapter 31
Sailing

Down the coast of England we sailed, the convoy now smaller, for ships were leaving formation, headed for various ports. After several days of numerous destroyer escorts, sea watches, meals, and sleep, we entered the harbor at Southampton. There was a flurry of activity on the docks as well as the shore. The convoy included countless ships of various kinds: freighters, tankers, destroyers, troop ships, tugboats, and sea-going tugs like the one I was on, ships that were designed to serve various purposes but all to help in the destruction of the opposing forces.

Several weeks before the invasion, things were happening. Airplanes, B-24's and B-17's (Flying Fortress) were flying over, headed across the English Channel, for France and Germany, loaded with explosives. Each plane had four large gasoline powered engines. There were hundreds of planes, and the cumulative sound of all of those engines was deafening, even though they were thousands of feet above us and it was a distant ten to fifteen minutes of flying time before they arrived over our area.

When they arrived over our area, the daylight which

D. Farrel – C. Woolsey – F. Antilla, 1944

A Dane shipmate and St's or small tugs.

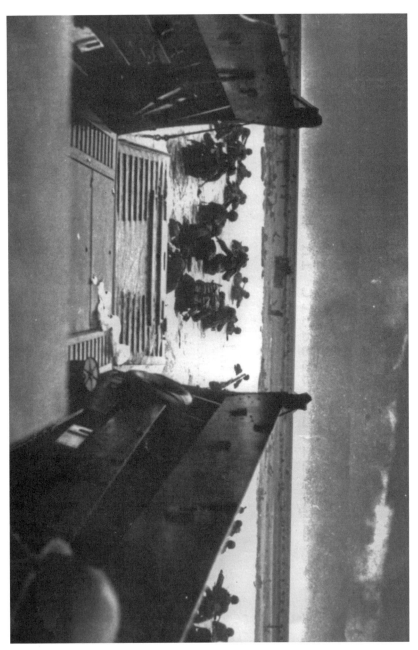

D-Day June 6, 1944

one had viewed just a few minutes before, had vanished. This darkness was caused by hundreds of heavy bombers, loaded with explosives, flown wing to wing, blocking out the rays of the sun. The sight and the sounds were both impressive and frightening, for they were on a death and destruction mission to Germany.

The allies were now the victors and not the victims. The end of WW II was in sight, spelling out the inability of humans to exist in peace, and the futility and waste of internecine wars. The passing airplanes blocked out the light for fifteen minutes, which seemed like hours. This became a daily occurrence.

It was the final bombing run for many of the crews. The vagaries of war and life. The Allies had recently initiated daylight bombing. An efficient, more accurate method of destruction than night bombing. It was an effective strategy, but costly. It was said that the Air Force bombing crews had a seventy-five percent casualty rate.

Chapter 32
Allied Invasion

Then it happened: Allies invade France June 6, 1944. And our work started: towing loaded barges, cranes, floating platforms and auxiliary bridges. We were busy. The first voyage across the English Channel was exciting.

We anticipated seeing the sites of the invasion and the country of France. The English Channel was cluttered with Allied warships, so we felt reasonably safe from German submarine activity. However, personally seeing as well as hearing "mess hall stories" of ship sinkings caused by enemy torpedoes and floating mines delivered by crews of enemy ships, told us a different story. The war was not yet over. Danger was still confronting us, sometimes every day. The enemy's discipline to carry out orders, regardless of the stage of their losing war, made it that way.

The coast of France came into view, which brought on thoughts of European history, grade school geography and limited knowledge of France and Europe. The world objected to the new geography that the German leaders envisioned, hence WW II, and the reason we were there. We positioned and secured our barge to a makeshift dock, and contemplated the day's happenings amidst the not-too-distant sounds of war.

On the nearby cliffs were ominous-looking, silent, vacated German fortifications overlooking the sea. Gray, circular, rounded top, humps of cement, about the size of a small house, with narrow horizontal openings, inches from the ground and facing the ocean. They were called German pillboxes. Looking up at them, it was easy to imagine, helmeted German soldiers peering down on the beaches with machine guns, small cannons, and automatic rifles sticking out of the horizontal slots.

It took courage, fortitude and a strong inner philosophy to disembark off a safe and comfortable ship, climb down rope ladders, with a full pack on your back, into waiting, pitching crowded and uninviting landing barges with sounds of nearby cannon and rifle fire and seeing the probability of dying, right in front of you. Soldiers being raked over into the water and beaches by enemy rifle and machine gun fire. The allied invasion of France, taking place. An amazing feat. Soldiers that have my admiration and gratitude.

With time on our hands and the ship waiting for orders, curiosity brought the crew up the hill-like cliff, to check out the German pillboxes. They appeared as if they were vacated just minutes before we got there.

There were bullets of all sizes, some of them the size used for hunting deer in Minnesota, and the other, the size of large salamis. There were boxes of hand-grenades and "potato mashers." "Potato Mashers" looked like a can of beans with a hammer handle attached to the center, making for a "t" like image. Both the grenades and the "potato mashers" were loaded with deadly, killing power.

Sacks and containers were filled with all three of these "souvenirs" that had been and still were, deadly German weapons, and were carried down and onto our ship. They were now unwisely, yet creatively and dangerously being put to other uses. The large shells were dismantled, the powder being taken out, and the lead put back in place—a shell without any detonating explosive powder. Two of these "dismantled" shells on a sanded piece of wood made exotic end pieces to a picture frame.

The grenades and the "potato mashers" were being employed in an off-season fourth of July celebration, with loud noises and the visual explosions in the water. Pull a pin on the grenade, and throw into the water and, in a few seconds, an underwater explosion. Unscrew the cap on the handle of the "potato masher," pull out the cord until you felt resistance, then steadily pull another quarter inch and throw into the sea, and shortly there was an explosion and a visual underwater action.

It took only a few of these explosions and the excited voices of the crew to bring the Captain and deck officers out to investigate. Loud voices and harsh words and the command came for all crew members assemble on the after deck. A search followed into all the lockers and likely hiding places for the German contraband. The "souvenirs" they found were enough in quantity to sink our ship, and the likelihood of an accidental explosion, was dangerously present. The "souvenirs" were thrown into the ocean and then a lecture came in angry, strong language, including equally strong, believable consequences for any future infractions.

Our ship continued towing equipment for all the Allied forces, including cranes, barges, disabled ships and equipment. The location of the ports we went to were constantly changing as the war progressed— Omaha and Utah beachheads, Cherbourg, Morlaix and Le Harve, France, and Ghent, Belgium. The English ports we sailed out of were Southampton, Plymouth, Liverpool, Cardiff, Swansea and Portsmouth.

Shore leave was looked forward to. The older seasoned sailors gave themselves and others a lively portrayal of uninhibited, alcoholic induced behavior.

Half and half (ale), rum and gin in England, cognac, calvados and wine in France, and friendly girls completed the anticipated "shore leave." It was a time of character transformation for some; for others, it was a continuation of a familiar life.

Chapter 33
Ship's Visitors & a Trip to Shore

On one trip when there was not any room at the dock, we were anchored offshore of Morlaix, France when an old French sailboat, with sails that had been patched over many times, pulled alongside of our ship. An older man in his 70s was at the rudder, busy handling lines, lowering sails and his eyes, surveying our gunwale for a place to secure his boat to our ship, for he had business to do.

The old captain was dressed in a patched shirt, pants and a discolored, worn sailor's cap with a damaged brim, clothes that had unmistakably been purchased before the war. The patches on his shirt and pants had worn through, exposing his skin. Some of the patches had a smaller patch sewed over the hole of the larger patch. The cloth used for the patches were of different colors—and then my eyes came down to his shoes!

They were wooden with stains of dubious origin; scarred with abrasions accumulated over the years. In place of stockings, he had hay and straw stuffed into his wooden shoes, that reached up and into the lower part of his tattered pant legs. Basic needs had been met, warmth and eventual replacement easily took place and with minimal cost. The impression of this man's appearance created a memory that has stayed with me.

Four smiling teenaged girls, probably his family or village girls, accompanied him. The girls were also catching the eyes of us seamen working on deck. The older man was intent on buying sorts of merchandise, speaking limited English, combined with gestures and basic French words. Clothing, sheets and especially cigarettes were traded underhandedly in exchange for French francs.

The trading finally ended, and now, the old captain had a different kind of a proposition. Anyone desiring to go ashore could do so with minimal cost, a candy bar or two, or a package of cigarettes. Three of us decided to take him up on his offer, thinking that a return trip to the ship would be readily available. Even though, the war was being fought close by, the thought of an adventure outweighed the risk. We surreptitiously climbed into the boat, and with a slight wind, our captain managed to sail at angles (tacking) up this wide river, to the little village of Morlaix. A time-consuming one way journey of several hours was the beginning of many thoughts that I would have of the wisdom of going ashore.

We finally arrived at an old rickety dock area, and I

should add, that we could hear the sound of heavy cannon fire that was taking place nearby. What am I doing here began to plague my thoughts. Well, we can go right back, I assured myself. We followed "the captain" up a worn gravel road to a small village. We could sense and see that we were quite a curiosity. Passersby were staring at us and talking excitedly in their native tongue. We could see a movement of curtains, people peeking out of windows, doorways and other places.

We finally arrived at an old house and we followed "the captain" inside. He briefly called his wife's attention to us with a sweep of his hand. His wife was about the same age as "the captain," wearing a worn, wrinkled dress. Facial expressions being revealing, I took comfort in her soothing look of gratitude at seeing Americans close up and having them as guests in her home.

Everything else had a strangeness and uncertainty about it. The dirt floors, aged walls and worn primitive furniture and strangers talking in a language we could not understand, surrounded us.

We were looking at the expressions on each of their aged faces, hoping to get a glimmer of what was going on. "The captain" motioned us to a rough wooden table, and we followed his example by sitting down. The wife and one of the girls (the others had apparently gone home) brought over bowls of dark broth. No bread. The broth had very little taste and had no body (thickness), and no second helpings were offered. I was a big eater and hungry. Silently I thought, this is no time to be fussy, better eat the broth, taste or no taste. Any port in a storm.

After supper, it seemed that I had become the spokesman for the three of us, so I addressed the captain, with motions and the English words, "Go back to the ship, <u>now</u> seel voo plaix?" (please in French) "Non demain," (no, tomorrow) was the response. Urgently, I repeated my request. "Back to ship, <u>now</u>. Seel voo plaix?" "Non, demain," he responded. "Cushe' here. (sleep here)." I guess we blew it, I thought. There will be hell to pay for missing a watch, and going ashore with out permission.

We did not know it, but "the captain" had other plans for us that evening. He gestured for the three of us to follow him and his wife. We went to a small building in the village center. It was packed with French people. Words were spoken in French as a sort of introduction of us three Americans. Then the people individually came to us, shook hands and spoke a few words of French, including "merci bowkoo" (thanks much) with a warm, ingratiating smile.

We returned to the "captain's" home and beds were found for us. Mine was a built-in bunk, like on a ship. The other two were quartered elsewhere. The girl (I am not sure what her relationship was to the old man and his wife) came over to my bunk, and gave me a goodnight kiss, and with a few French words, blew out the candle and left. Her kiss made all the problems we were starting to experience worthwhile.

Early the next morning, "the captain" woke us up, and the four of us walked down to the boat. After several hours of tacking to catch the wind in the wide river, we found ourselves in the proximity of where our boat had been. It was gone! On the distant horizon was a profile of a ship that might have been ours. I directed "the captain" to shore. After a handshake and a wave, "the captain" set his sails homeward. And we went in search of the U.S. Army Port Captain.

Chapter 34
Sailing on Dutch Ship

We found the Port Captain, and explained what had happened. He had the necessary travel papers made out and had a jeep take us to an old small Dutch ship that was leaving for England. The ship was built around 1890. The old diesel engine pushed the ship at about 3-4 knots (approximately 5 mph) which the ship's cook discovered was about trolling speed. After his galley work was done, he would go on the stern and fish. He caught enough cod to feed the crew. He prepared it in an unforgettable, delectable way.

To pass the time, I volunteered to stand a sea-watch on the steering wheel, steering the ship, getting my direction from the previous helmsman or the deck officer on watch, using an old magnetic brass compass to steer by. The ship was so ancient, that it had ropes running from the wheel to the rudder. The bow of the boat had a wide swing as it proceeded and plowed through the sea toward England, a swing of approximately 25 degrees.

So, eventually I got accustomed to the constant swing, by steering a course with equal number of degrees on each side of the given compass course. Because of our slow speed, we would have been an

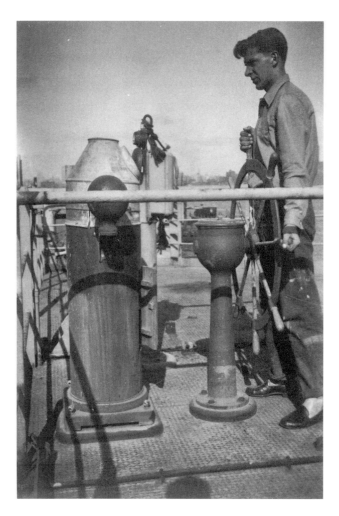

Frank on the ship's wheel.

Frank Antilla coming on board.

ideal target for any submarine. There were interesting conversations with the deck officer on watch and also the captain, who I suspect spent much time in the wheel house on my watch, just for talking purposes. They were as interested in the U.S.A., as I was in their country and Europe.

Chapter 35
Back on Board

We docked at an English port and then boarded a train to Southampton, where we boarded our ship. The Captain showed his displeasure with choice words, as well as docking our pay.

Occasionally, when the docks were in use (full), occupied with various kinds of ships, newly arriving ships entering the harbor had to find other ways to secure their ships, so that they would have the protection of the harbor. They had to either drop anchor in mid harbor, or tie up to a buoy, when they were available. The floating buoys were secured by a massive chain attached to a heavy anchor that was lying on the bottom of the sea.

Regrettably, because of indulging in a alcoholic beverage concoction, some of the crew members had made, I had the misfortune of falling overboard when my ship was tied up to a buoy in an English port with a surging outgoing tide taking place. The top of the gunwale (sides) of the seagoing tugboat was approximately six feet above the surface of the water. Fully clothed, the outgoing tide started carrying me to the entrance of the harbor and the ocean. Luckily, while I had lived on Lawrence Lake, I had become a

Heading out to sea.

On board small tug.

strong swimmer, so I went into an overhand stroke, and my feet, with shoes on churning the sea with a powerful forward thrust.

I was making headway against the outgoing tide and soon got close enough to the ship to grab the end of a wood mop handle that a shipmate had extended. Soon, the strong arms of our Norwegian captain pulled the scrawny, skinny kid that had had too much to drink to his angry eye level. I remember being slammed in the face by an open hand or closed fist and laid on the deck with sea water and vomit pouring out of my mouth. Before losing consciousness, I thought, thank God, I will never do that again.

Chapter 36
Towing British Crane to Antwerp, December 1944

In mid-1944, in order to get out of sight of the withering, unforgiving eye of the captain who had saved me from dire circumstances, I had the opportunity to transfer to another seagoing tug, The LT 363, that had an opening for an able seaman. The LT 363 had a wooden hull, and was about the same size as the LT 532, the ship that I had gotten off of. I got the 4-8 watch, which was the captain's watch. The 4-8 was a desirable watch, in that the sleeping hours were closer to normal (at night) and then one's off hours were daylight. So I considered my transferring to another ship a stroke of luck.

We continued to tow materials across the English Channel. The war was progressing. Then in the early part of December 1944, we received orders to tow a British crane and crew to Antwerp, Belgium. The stories and rumors were that we would be the first allied ship to enter the Belgium port of Antwerp, which was laden with floating mines, by the retreating Germans. An unknown to our crew, was that "The Battle Of The Bulge" and the battle and battles of Bastogne (which was twenty miles from Antwerp) would be taking place December 1944.

We had left England and were steaming towards Antwerp. We had no escort, and we saw an occasional ship. An ominous sight came into view, an abandoned small rubber life raft with an American flag on a makeshift staff floated by. When we got to the coast of Belgium and started proceeding inland, we started seeing green wreck buoys.

The purpose of the wreck buoys, were to mark sunken vessels that were at various depths below the surface of the water and a danger to navigation. The amount of water that covered the sunken ship was undetermined and constantly changing, because of tide and other factors. Sunken ships at times had cavities of air making them semi-buoyant, subject to movement by currents and underwater movement, allowing a sunken ship to move from a marked position (green buoy) to a traffic lane that had moving ships.

Right after the change of watch, I was on the steering wheel, staring at a small patch of light on the gyro-compass. Captain Christenson was at the front wheel house window peering ahead into the darkness. The other AB seaman on watch was outside on the wing of the wheel house, also looking into the darkness for lights or anything unusual to report to the captain. The British crane, with its crew of men was following behind, held in tow by a 4 inch steel cable. Suddenly, the ship lurched and started climbing upward, as if we were sliding upward on a slanted piece of a rock, which in actuality was a submerged floating ship that had drifted into the traffic lane.

Captain Christenson ran back to what is called the telegraph, a ship's communication system with the engine room. He swung the brass telegraph handle from an area denoting full speed ahead to a marked area that states full speed astern. This movement on the wheelhouse telegraph is viewed as an order and thus confirmed by the engine room. They would repeat the exact change on the engine room telegraph, which is then viewed on the wheelhouse telegraph.

The two telegraphs and the procedure that is used guarantee the certainty of the orders given. The propeller direction is quickly reversed, causing the ship to shudder and to slowly start moving backward. Meanwhile, the crane continues its forward movement, in the direction in which it was being towed and an inevitable crash is forthcoming.

The moving crane hit our backing ship on the starboard side splintering the heavy wood timbers. Because of the uncertainty of additional damage to the ship's bottom and keel, we tied up to a nearby buoy to wait for daylight. The captain and I remained in the wheelhouse peering into the darkness and waiting for daylight and our watch to end.

Chapter 37
German E-Boat Encounter

Looking into the darkness, your eyes make an adjustment that acclimate your ability to see at night. Peering out the window, an unbelievable sight was starting to take place. A German E-Boat slowly came into view. A German E-boat has a similar profile to our PT boat and the Canadian Corvette, thereby making it easily identifiable. It is a sleek, fast, maneuverable and deadly attack vessel. The German boat circled our ship and crane several times. The sound of their engine exhaust and the profile of their vessel suggested its power and advanced capability.

Our captain's thoughts were unreadable in the dark wheelhouse. They were probably similar to my own. What are they going to do? Shell the wheel house, the command center of our ship, even though we were only a humble sea-going tug boat, with no guns or armor in view? At times, when they were circling our ship, the reflection of greenish light from their instrument panel, revealed the outline of crew members, which made the scenario more fearful. All of a sudden, their throttles were slammed full ahead; we knew this because their vessel lurched into an almost vertical position as they roared off into the night. Their decision to leave saved our ship, and very likely, our lives.

Come daylight we proceeded to the sea port of Antwerp, Belgium. After dropping off the British crane, we proceeded to Berth #192. The sound effects from both the German and Allied Armies were evident. The Battles of the Bulge, Bastogne, Belgium were taking place. We felt reasonably safe, because that was at least twenty miles away.

Chapter 38
Ship Hit by German Missile

We felt safe until we became aware of low flying German rockets overhead. We recognized the rocket by its profile and the sound of its small four-cycle engine. Its sound that was similar to an American Briggs and Stratton auxiliary engine, an engine that had a variety of uses in the states such as motorized scooters and washing machines.

The Germans had attached this small, similar engine to an explosive rocket. For fuel, they metered the gasoline in exact proportions. When the fuel supply was depleted, the bomb came down and exploded. The gas usage and the distance traveled were determined mathematically, unless there was a communication setup involving collaborators who could supply underhanded information that would make the rocket droppings and their explosions more accurate.

I was standing on the bow of the LT 363 watching and counting the rockets flying overhead. There were approximately 50 every hour. They were landing and exploding close by. As I was staring up into the sky, a rocket was over the ship, and the engine stopped. I ran into the mess hall, where some of the crew were

playing cards and talking. I opened the door and
shouted, "There's a V-1 over the ship, and it's coming
down." The place: Antwerp, Belgium, Berth 192, the
date: December 29, 1944. The time: 3:15 p.m.

I had noticed that U.S. Army engineers had been
digging a trench on the dock area. I thought, if I
could get into this trench, I would be below the
surface of the ground, and therefore be protected
from concussion and blast. Apparently others had the
same idea, because they were in my way when I tried
to get off the ship.

I waited a bit, and then managed to get on the dock.
I was running for the trench, but I never made it. The
V-1 hit and exploded approximately 50 feet from me.
There was a horrendous explosion and I felt myself
being propelled upward for what seemed like about
15 feet and then I came down, and pieces of dirt and
debris kept dropping with me and on me. My ears
were screaming. The immediate space and sky was
full of heavy dust I thought and felt like I had been
killed.

I continued lying there in shock, covered with dirt
and debris. I felt someone grasping and pulling me
up out of my burial blanket and asking, "Are you all
right?" Shortly, they had numerous jeeps that they
loaded the whole crew into. They told us that we were

being taken to a hospital to get checked over.

Unknown to us crew members, the Germans had been dropping German soldiers, dressed in American Army uniforms, and trained to speak in an America accent. Because of that, the Americans had road blocks every couple of miles. A half-dozen American soldiers would approach the jeeps with guns drawn.

They would open both doors and ask all occupants, not for identification tag or papers, but with verbal questions to each individual: Who is Mickey Mouse? What state is Chicago in? Where is the Empire State Building located? In our jeep, we had an older Norwegian engineer who could barely speak English. They took him out of the jeep in an unkindly, but officious manner, handcuffed and brought him into their guard shack.

Chapter 39
The Hospital

We finally got to this large building that was regarded as a hospital. The building seemed to be unheated, and we could hear the German rockets flying overhead and nearby explosions, besides other distant sounds that sounded like cannon fire. All of us were shivering from cold, shock and fear as they looked at our bodies and into our ears, accompanied with questions.

We were told that the army regarded the V-1 rocket explosion that we had experienced on our ship as a direct hit. Each crewman's hometown newspaper was sent a descriptive accounting of the explosion. My hometown news, "The Bovey Press," sent a copy to The Iron Range Museum, located at Chisholm, Minnesota. It is there and supposedly always will be. (1945 archives)

Chapter 40
Ship Damage, Tow to England

Back to the ship. The damage from the blast was extensive. Wood was caved in. Our wheelhouse was flattened, the windows gone. The concussion and movement had somehow damaged our diesel engine so that it was not operable. Canvas was nailed over the wheel house openings. Makeshift repairs were implemented.

While doing these repairs, for some reason they repositioned our ship to a different berth. Shortly after this repositioning was completed, a German V-1 rocket came down and exploded in exactly in the same place where our ship had been, Berth #192. This suggested behind-the-lines collaborative activity.

Another seagoing tugboat was dispatched, and we were towed back to Southampton, England. The LT 363 was a sorry sight. It looked like it had been though several wars, and lost them both. We arrived in Southampton and had to go through several locks to get to the designated area.

The locks were manned by Limeys. And apparently the sight of the damaged and decrepit LT 363, being towed, caused the workers to break out in shouts, cheers and clapping, which made all of us feel like the conquering heroes returning home. It was an appreciated and emotional welcome. There were not many dry eyes among the crew. The welcome was their way of expressing gratitude for the visible effects our ship displayed of enemy confrontation and survival The memory of the event, will always be with me. We then packed our belongings into our sea bags and vacated our previous home, the battered LT 363.

We then received orders to proceed to Liverpool, England. The word was out that tugboats designed for harbor or river work (without a keel) were being sent across the Atlantic Ocean on the decks of freighters. They were sent to Liverpool because a large American crane, capable of lifting them off the decks of the freighters and placing them in the water, was stationed there. Our new assignment was going to be to man these harbor tugboats and deliver them to designated ports in France, Belgium, and Holland.

Chapter 41
Travel Through England

The American crane at Liverpool—huge and capable of being rigged to pick up various size lifts—was an awesome sight. Backside of the crane was a sampling of American G.I. humor. In large letters scrolled with an artistic touch were the words: "Five minutes walk and you con't miss it, the E.T.O. war cry."(The E.T.O. was the European Theatre of Operations.) This was a fun statement, whether you were American or British. There were many American servicemen in England, and the streets were full of them, walking here or there, thus it was commonplace for the G.I.s to ask and for the British to give them directions.

It was an opportune time for the British to capitalize on this American quirk and have a little humor in the tense and stressful time of war. "How does one get here or get there?" was a typical inquiry. Their response to this question was usually given with "tongue in cheek," or with the flavor of whimsical exaggeration like, "Tell you what chap, go this way, bear to the left/right and it's about a five minute walk, and you con't miss it."

At times, the G.I. would find himself further away, rather than arriving at the destination. After receiving, repeated similar directions, he would catch on, and consider all directions with skepticism, humor and with an adjustment factor. Fun.

Small harbor tug deliveries to ports in France and Belgium continued and then we would be relieved by a U.S. Army tugboat crew, and we would go back to England, usually transported on a U.S. Navy LST, and eventually get back to Liverpool and crew another harbor tugboat and again bring it across the English Channel.

The itinerary in getting to Liverpool was, take a train to London, and then a train from London to Liverpool, a fun trip because of the various diversions. Interesting views, castles, people, besides many drinking establishments and girls.

Chapter 42
The Tug

We arrived in Liverpool and immediately we were put on a brand new ST. An ST was an acronym for small tug. Being on a small tug had its advantages. The quarters were comfortable and the small tugs always worked in harbors, which meant, that the crew was always in port, where all the action is, not at sea, for extended periods. Usually, the harbor work was done in daylight hours. But our job was delivering the small tugs. That involved constant change: deliver the boat across the channel, then go back to Liverpool for another delivery.

The crews got to be good friends. We were on a small ship, so, there was only so much room. This small size created a lot of interaction, at work, mealtime and going ashore, looking for art galleries, museums, dissertations on culture and other activities that were of interest to sailors. The misinformation in the preceding sentence was the author's vain attempt to add humor to the page. Many of the seamen were repeatedly assigned to the same small tug over and over again. That way, we got to know one another quite well. We had already worked with one and another on previous deliveries.

Chapter 43
Dave Farrel

I got to be good friends with one of the seamen, Dave Farrel from eastern Pennsylvania. His brother John had died on the Bataan Death March. He was from a family of three additional brothers and one sister; he was the youngest. He was about two years older than me and was tall and muscular. Dave had the reputation of never backing away from a fight, and never losing one either.

We were walking down the street one time, and some GI's were going in the opposite direction. One of them turned around and ran back to talk to Dave. He said that in peacetime, he was a fight promoter, and he was looking for what the boxing world calls a "white hope." That is white fellows in the heavy weight class who would be interested in a career of developing into a prize fighter. Dave was flattered at being asked, and gave him an address to contact "after the war considerations."

Chapter 44
A Motorcycle

Dave and I talked to Captain Patterson, the skipper of this particular small tug that we were on, about getting and keeping a motorcycle on the ship. He told us if we kept it on the ship and used it in a responsible way, we had his permission. We went shopping. We found a 1938 Triumph. A noted British motorcycle, it was gutty, fast and could take a lot of punishment with minimal maintenance. We paid the garage forty-two English pounds for it ($168.00 in USA currency).

We managed to get the small amount of fuel we needed from our friend, the ship's chief engineer. We had to get used to driving on the left hand side of the road. We got a traffic violation connected to driving on the left-hand side, and were given a traffic ticket. We gave the Bobby (English policeman) our ship's address.

Getting mail was an unpredictable event, because sometimes weeks and even month passed before our mail caught up with us. Much later, we were in a French port and our mail arrived. In our mail, was a letter containing a summons to appear in "His Majesty's Court." The date that we were to appear had long passed. We did not get any further communication, so I assume, all is well in "his majesty's court."

Chapter 45
Deliver Small Tugboats

We continued to deliver small tugs to ports that were close to where the war was being fought. At times, we remained on our boats for days or weeks before we were relieved or ordered to depart for England.

At times the port we were in was near to cannon fire, ours and theirs. The Germans had a weapon that they called 88s. We called them "screaming meemies" because, first there was an explosion (a hit) and the screaming sound came afterwards, for the projectile was faster than the sound. The German V-1 rocket that had demolished the LT-363 continued to be used against us and they were dropping and exploding at times and places when they were least expected.

The crew would go ashore in the midst of the fringe areas where war was being fought a few miles inland. Staying on the ship was as dangerous as going ashore. Occasionally, in our meanderings, we would pass by a building or street where a German projectile had recently hit. We would see the effects of the explosion: wreckage, fire, smoke, injured people and people stumbling around wild eyed, in shock.

Chapter 46
War and Other Things

In a world of war, and being the youngest crew member of merchant marine ships that I sailed on, I observed the mannerisms of other seamen, good or bad. They talked about getting drunk and getting into fights. They talked about sexual conquests after every shore leave. I was not an innocent young man; the seaman's world that I now lived in made sure of that.

A particular time comes back to remind me of youth, foolishness and behavior that makes me have reservations about including the incident in this book, but here goes. Dave and I were walking down the street when we met two women going the opposite direction. Apparently they were lonely, for they had a warm, friendly smile. "Bonjour Mademoiselle," Dave greeted them, using the French greeting words. French is an international language, even though we were in the country of Belgium. We received an immediate response, "Bonjour Monsieur."

The verbal communication was limited, but their friendship was unmistakable. The next thing, the four of us were walking in the same direction, smiling, laughing, like we were old acquaintances, from a previous time. Communication included bits of French, Flemish and English, with gestures and warm, accepting smiles.

The next thing, we were climbing a stairway, leading to an apartment entrance. The communication with one another became more intimate, and soon the four of us were in a large, double bed. We spent the night there, with the sound of rockets, projectiles of various intensities, landing around us. Some were close and others were of varying distances. We were oblivious to the apparent danger. It was a secondary interest.

Chapter 47
A Delivery to the Mediterranean

Our arrival in Liverpool this time was different. There were seven new harbor tugboats already in the water, waiting for their crews. The highly secretive orders were soon common news. All seven tugs were to be sailed to Marseilles, France. We were to be escorted by two British destroyers. The plan was to sail across the English Channel, and cross the Bay of Biscay, that was off the coast of France, and head south. We would be sailing by the coast of Spain and Portugal. Any kind of stoppage there would have meant internment, for they were neutral countries, as well as Spain having a fascist leaning. Leave the Atlantic Ocean, proceed through the Straits of Gibraltar into the Mediterranean Sea and into the southern French port of Marseilles.

It was exciting news, because of the different geographic area, southern France and the Mediterranean Sea. The seven tugs were in a formation designated by the British destroyers. The small tugs were in constant radio contact with each other as well as the destroyers. The American radio communications with one other ship was typically laced with obscenities as well as other four-letter words. The content of their communications was a gross departure from Lord Fauntleroy's dictum or formal military propriety.

153

These communications continued on until a crisp woman's voice interrupted one of the typical radio conversations: "Gentlemen, from now on, you will refrain from any further communications on his majesty's airways until you remember to talk like the gentlemen that you are." Her admonishment was effective because radio communications on the small tugboats became devoid of the former earthy flavor.

We sailed down the coast of England until we were close to a point of land jutting out into the Atlantic Ocean. A point of land called Land's End. Suddenly the moderate fog intensified along with the approaching nightfall. Visibility became difficult and further sailing dangerous. The Atlantic was calm and our request to anchor for the night was granted.

Our small ship's anchor system was not designed like the larger ships. Our anchor was secured to the forward deck, so we secured a heavy steel cable to it and physically lift it up over the gunwale and drop it into the sea. Let out enough slack and secure the cable to a cleat on the ship. Satisfied that the ship would be secure for the night, we all went into the galley for supper.

The room that we ate in included both the large cook stove, wall cabinets and counter with enough stools to seat the entire crew. While we were chowing down and taking part in rambling conversations, we felt a heavy jarring sensation as if someone had pulled the drain plug of the ocean and drained the water, for it felt like the ship was now aground. The captain ran up the ladder into the wheelhouse and to the engine room controls and the chief engineer hurried down into the engine room.

It was too late. The crew got outside just as the anchor cable broke. The tide was receding rapidly. The captain was signaling the engine room for power, so we could go out with the tide into deeper water. The propeller was turning and digging up ocean sand. It was too late. Our ship was doing a balancing act trying to keep from falling over on its side. But to no avail. The ship teetered and came crashing down, lying on its side on the floor of the Atlantic Ocean.

It was not only embarrassing to the captain, but he now had new fears that the ship would not right herself in the incoming tide, and fill up with water and meet her demise and remain in Davey Jones' locker. We lowered our life boat, just in case the ocean bottom would not release the sand imbedded ship's side.

Luckily, again, the good Lord looked down on us with favor. The tide came surging back. We were all holding our breath when the bubbles first appeared and the small tug slowly righted herself to a normal position.

The captain decided that perhaps we may have bent our propeller shaft, so we proceeded to a nearby port, Tenby, England. Shore leave was permitted, so the crew headed for an American Red Cross Club, housed in an old, leased English hotel.

The club was packed with servicemen from other war ships and nearby camps. English ladies of various ages dispensed tea, eats and conversations. An ancient piano, with a G.I., that had taken his piano lessons seriously, was on the key-board. Soon many of us were gathered around the piano as old favorites like "Twelfth Street Rag," "Sweet Lorraine" and other old and current hits rolled off his finger tips. The songs brought back stateside memories of youthful pursuits of recent years. It was a great evening.

The ship had been checked over and in daylight hours we started across the English Channel. In several days, we were off the coast of Portugal, traveling southward. The weather was a departure from the cold, rain, and dampness of the seaports of central Europe. Every day was noticeably warmer. One day, Dave Farrel and I were sitting on the stern, soaking up the sunshine, and talking about this and that, when Dave said, "I think I'm going to hang onto a rubber tire fender along side of the ship to cool off."

I was somewhat taken back, for it did not sound like a

sensible or safe thing to do, but I thought, Dave should realize the seriousness and the danger involved. Our small tug had its place in the small convoy of seven ships, as well as the two British destroyers. Full speed ahead was the standing order.

Dave lowered himself into the refreshing water. His face reflects his enjoyment as the water splashes over his large physique. A few minutes went by, and I felt uneasy with big Dave hanging onto the tire-fender. Pretty soon I was prompted to say, "You had better pull yourself back on board." When I could see that his effort to do that was of no avail, I shouted at him, "Hey Dave, whatsa matter, can't you do it?" He returned no answer. I realized the dangerous predicament that was manifesting itself. Dave weighed over two hundred pounds, and if his strength failed, he could slip downward into the ship's propeller area and be chewed up and disabled.

I quickly climbed the ladder to the wheelhouse and shouted to Captain Battersby, "Shut the engine off, Dave is over the side of the ship hanging onto a tire-fender." Captain Battersby instantly shut the engine off and he and other members of the crew came down, and we pulled, yanked and tugged "Big Dave" back onto the ship.

Meanwhile, one of the British destroyers saw our

tug slow to a near stop, started signaling by radio as well as in Morse Code with their ship's light, "What is problem, urgent. Area is operating grounds for German submarines. Answer." We answered by resuming normal speed. Other explanations would have been too embarrassing. Dave never mentioned his conference with the Captain and the Chief Engineer. Dave experienced a lucky break and a lesson in growing up.

Our next stop was Gibraltar, an old British fortress. It was of historical importance, because the fortress determined what ships left or entered the Mediterranean Sea. If need be, any ship could easily be destroyed and sunk by the huge cannons that bristled on all sides of "The Rock" as it was commonly called. The place was teeming with British servicemen, sailors and soldiers alike. England's war with the Fascists had started in 1939 and now it was 1944. Many of the service people had been there that long. They were burdened with oncoming stories of the abundance of Americans (yanks) in the homeland and their amorous and successful pursuits. Hence, there was an understandable hostility.

Our seven harbor tugboats pulled into Gibraltar for refueling and repairs and to take on supplies. Stories of good food, quality booze at very reasonable prices, free freshly caught shrimp in the most frequented

Rock of Gibralter.

ST (Small Tug)

bars, fresh fruit of many kinds peddled on stands in the streets and horse-drawn carriage rides. All of these things were at unbelievable low prices. Stories like this drifted back to the ships. Regrettably, drinking and booze is at the top of a sailor's priorities and nothing brings out the brashness and ill-begotten manners of anyone like intoxication.

The drunken behavior of the sailors from the tugboats was not well received. It was with pleasure that the anger of the British servicemen could be vented, resulting in black eyes, bruises, and missing teeth. For some of my shipmates and seamen from the other tugboats, Gibraltar will remain a bad memory.

The weather turned nasty as we entered the Mediterranean Sea. The wind started increasing in intensity, creating huge waves and increasing the danger to the small harbor tug boats. A harbor tugboat is built like a bath tub so that it can operate in shallow, harbors. The marine architects or designers had no idea that there was a possibility of them being sailed on the oceans of the world.

We were sailing towards Marseilles, France and the winds were increasing in intensity and making dangerous waves. The tugs were reasonably safe as long as the bows were pointed squarely into the waves. The waves would cause the ship to pitch up and down.

Danger developed whenever the ship got into the trough of the waves with the bow being parallel to the waves. This would cause the ship to roll from port to starboard (left to right) As that happened, some ships would roll over so far that they would be laying on their side, with water pouring through the smoke stack, and sinking the tug. Because of the storm and the wind, the boats lost their formation and the word came that the British destroyers picked up some crew members from the warm Mediterranean waters, regrettably, not all.

Meanwhile, our small tug was pitching bow up, bow down. Our gunwales were full of water, causing the sea water to flow into the crew's cabins as well as the galley and engine room. Dave Farrel and I shared the last cabin on the port side. Our cabin had two bunks, storage lockers, and a desk. I had the bottom bunk, and my water-soaked mattress would rise and fall with the movement and sloshing of the water in the cabin. Clothing, blankets, phonograph records and other things floating around the room made us realize the seriousness of the moment.

Because we had to keep the bow pointed into the waves, we could not change course to proceed to Marseilles, with the certainty of capsizing, if we did change course. The captain decided that for reasons of safety for the tugboat and crew, we would proceed to the small island of Corsica. The island and protective harbor were in alignment with our course of direction. We steamed into the harbor with out mishap, and gratefully waited out the storm.

A French Corvette, a small maneuverable attack ship was tied up in the dock next to ours. Soon lively trading was taking place between the French sailors and our crew. Table wine for cigarettes, French francs for anything else. Lively bargaining discussions ensued. "Comme bien, how much Joe? You speak," uttered the Frenchman. The French called all Americans Joe. The American seaman, not sure about his French linguistics, would respond using the English words "you speak first." Mysteriously, the Frenchman would understand, and respond in French words for specific numbers, and helped out in the comprehension of the price, by holding the exact number of fingers, with his hand or both hands held aloft. Meanwhile some of the crew members were getting intoxicated by drinking excessive amounts of the recently traded table wine.

Thus our brief visit to the birthplace of Napoleon and the island of Corsica, came to an end. Several days later, with fair skies and seas we sailed to Marseille, France. Our stay in Marseille came to last several months because of the need for a tugboat and experienced crew. Besides the harbor work, towing this and that within the harbor, we enjoyed an interesting time, warm balmy weather, reasonably good cook and food on the ship, shore leave and the absence of German rockets and cannon fire.

Some of our spare time, when the ship wasn't working, was spent swimming from our dock and boat to the breakwater. It was a distance of a quarter mile or so. The ocean water was clear. The breakwater was also used by the French city people. They would walk on the huge rocks, and for some the huge breakwater rocks would be used for sunbathing. Swimming to the breakwater and back to the ship was and tiring. When we became fatigued in swimming that long distance, we would dog paddle until rested, then swim again.

By the time we got back to the ship, we were tired and hungry. Making lunch for all of us five to seven hungry seaman was a job. Someone would surreptitiously take most of the weakly meat allotment and make hamburgers or steak sandwiches. I often made the milk shakes, by combining powdered milk and powdered eggs, sugar, a heavy douse of vanilla, mixed in a huge aluminum pitcher with a heavy duty hand-powered whisk. Beat it, stir it, and make it as thick as I could. Then carry all of this food and beverage to the "flying bridge," (top of the wheelhouse) where we had some makeshift chairs. Eat, drink and talk. What a life. Those times were great stuff. The memories linger on.

Those times ended when we got orders to leave the ship and return back to Liverpool, England, and resume delivering small tugboats. Several years later, when I continued sailing in the peace time Merchant Marine, my ship, a freighter returned to Marseille with a load of coal (Marshall Plan). I went down to the same area in which we had been docked and found the small tug that I had crewed on. It now had a French crew and their flag on the mast halyard. The memories came rushing back. The word nostalgia does not satisfactorily explain how I felt, because it was more than that.

We delivered a few more STs. But as the war progressed, the need for STs diminished. Eventually we got orders to go to a place that was about thirty miles from Paris, France, that was called "Chatteau Noin Telle." It was a place where seamen stayed while they were waiting for re-assignment. Its most recent occupants had been a German Panzer Division. It was a relaxing change, in that all we had to do was eat, sleep and read, or to visit nearby Paris. I chose to read, and selected books out of our library, which was a room with many cardboard boxes, filled with books.

Chapter 48
Return Home

Soon, we were given the choice to return to the USA, or to sign a contract for an extended time period. I had been in Europe close to sixteen months, so I opted to return home. My friend Dave decided to sign another contract and stay, and so we parted ways. I returned to the USA on the U.S. Coast Guard troop transport, the USS General Black. We arrived in Boston, Massachusetts in August 1945. We were given a rousing welcome by local civic groups. Tug boats, firefighting boats loaded with bands, waving girls and other people. It was heartwarming.

I went home for several weeks, My mother had remarried. My stepfather gave me a receptive, warm welcome to his and now my mother's home. Now, I was no longer a crushed boy, looking for a father, or a home, or a house to live in. I was a mature young man, eighteen years old, with a life that was overflowing with experiences—experiences that had been both good and not as good.

My mother and stepfather were married for six years until his demise. After several weeks at home, I returned to an Eastern seaport and shipped out as an able seaman. I sailed rusty ships on the oceans

Leharve France, heading home, 08/15/45

Back from Europe, on leave 1945.

of the world. It was an interesting and enjoyable occupation.

I had been studying to take an examination for a third mate's license (deck officer). I had memorized "The Rules Of The Road," a lengthy explanation of a ship's navigation rules. My plan was to go to a Merchant Marine officer's school at Mobile, Alabama with emphasis on celestial navigation.

At the end of the course, I would take my written examination. Los Angelas Tankers Co. had a third mate's job waiting—I had sailed on one of their T-2 tankers, the SS Wolf Creek, as quartermaster where I became adept at both loading and unloading our petroleum cargo. My work ethic is and always has been, is productivity and "make yourself useful."

It was not only suggested, but urged by the first mate, the deck officer on my watch, that I write the examination and get a third mate's license. I still have the recommendation in my box of mementos, another memory of the past. However, I had decided to quit sailing on salt water. I was not cut out to be a lifetime sailor. Four years had been enough. I had been thinking of other possibilities to explore, so the third mate's job or license did not materialize.

Chapter 49
Merchant Marine Discharge
and Adventure

In the summer of 1947, I made my last voyage on salt water. We sailed a Liberty Ship, loaded with grain, to Youkasouka, Japan. On the return voyage, we went directly from Japan, to the Panama Canal, a voyage of thirty days. We proceeded to Galveston, Texas, where I was discharged in August 1947.

I went home and worked at several uninteresting jobs. I made the usual young person's activity circuit, which involved drinking, chasing girls, and automobiles. It was fun, but not satisfying. There has to be something more in life.

In this circle of friends, a young fellow, by the name of Charlie (Chuck) Oats and I became acquainted. He was quiet, unassuming young fellow, about twenty four years old. He had recently been discharged from The U.S. Army. He showed me a government-given certificate stating that he (Chuck) had been awarded a Silver Star decoration for bravery.

The certificate contained a detailed accounting. The event for which he was decorated took place in a battlefield setting, with intense fighting and

Deck cargo.

opposition from the enemy (German). Their pillbox and Wehrmacht soldiers were in the midst of this setting. It was strategically located to wipe out the advancing American infantry.

A pillbox is a cement fortification, with a dome covering. The curvature of the cement dome would deflect rifle as well as cannon hits. The dome had numerous rectangular openings. The openings were large enough to allow for visibility, as well as the thrusting and firing of various kinds of weaponry.

The certificate stated that Chuck Oats ran at the cement pillbox, firing his M-1 rifle at the pillbox as he ran; he was also carrying a grenade. Upon arriving at the pillbox, he threw himself on the ground in front of one the openings, and at the same time, pulled the pin on the grenade, and dropped it into the opening. Shortly an explosion occurred, and those German soldiers that were able to, scrambled out of exit opening carrying their weapons. Chuck shot them as they exited.

Outwardly, Chuck did not look or act like the hero that was being portrayed in the commendation. Chuck and I hit it off, and decided to travel to Alaska. A ship that I was crewmember on had stopped there in 1943. I thought it might be an opportune place and time to start a business. Chuck was uncertain about what he would do there, but he definitely wanted to go.

Some forgotten port.

Chapter 50
Berdie

We started out, stopping briefly at Minnesota, a place that held a storehouse of memories, both good and some that were not the best. On my short visit there, a year earlier, I had met a young girl who had a pleasing appearance and personality. Her name was Berdie Wivell. I called her up and let her know that I was back in Minnesota. I told her about my friend Chuck, and asked her if she could find one of her girlfriends for him to get acquainted with so the four of us could go out. Always a good organizer, Berdie had friends that would have welcomed the opportunity for a date with a returning veteran, especially one with hero status.

She arranged a date with a pretty girl named Bonnie. That date led to numerous dates that created additional memories for the four of us. Chuck fell for Bonnie, but apparently the feeling was not reciprocated, because nothing came of the chance meeting. They both eventually married other persons. Berdie and I did not. We married four year after we had met on July 11, 1951. Besides being a good organizer, she has been a good influence. Enough said.

Chapter 51
Western Adventure

Chuck and I left Minnesota, heading westward. We were driving a 1935 black Ford two-door sedan with a heater but no radio. It was old, but had low mileage, a snappy V-8 engine and it proved to be trouble free. We had a couple of sleeping bags and a camp stove. We slept out on the prairies of North Dakota and Montana. We cooked basic meals, beans, hotdogs, hamburgers on our camp stove—all amidst a lot of talk. They were good times.

Somewhere I had heard that there was good wages to be made in the forests of western Washington. So, why not acquire a little more cash before heading North to Alaska? A small logging town of Hoquiam, Washington became our interim destination. We immediately got jobs with Polson Logging Company as choker setters, a job that did not require much skill, but physical fitness and dexterity were a requisite. Because it was hard, rigorous work, there was a constant job turnover.

Polson Logging Company, Camp Six, was in The Olympic Mountain Range, seven miles from the Pacific Ocean. There were no roads going to the camp. The company had their own railroad. They used the impressive Malley Railroad Engine for hauling the logs out to saw mills and other places. They had a gasoline-powered speeder and a trailer with benches to haul their crews and supplies. The speeder and trailer had canvas tarps on the sides that could be dropped down when the weather was foul and rainy, which was most of the winter.

Polson Logging Company had several camps. Camp Fourteen was north of us and also close to the Pacific Ocean. "The landing," was approximately fifteen miles from Camp Six, a place where we parked our cars for the week or until we decided to go to town, or leave the camp entirely. It was also the designated place to get on the company speeder for the ride to camp.

Polson Logging Company was a big operation. Our camp had approximately 130 employees. Fallers, buckers, windfall buckers, hook tenders, rigging slingers, choker setters, whistle punks, saw filer, donkey punchers, tree-toppers, loaders and bull cooks. In addition there were the camp foreman, timber scalers, time keeper, and the kitchen crew, cooks, waiters, and kitchen flunkies.

They had ancient railroad cars for bunkhouses. There were seven men to a bunkhouse, with a huge wood burning stove on one end of the bunk house. The "bull-cooks" kept the bunkhouses clean, made our beds, kept the fires going in the stoves, and had the wood storage bin full of chopped wood.

Close to the stove were two gallon cans with the tops removed, full of kerosene. They had formerly held vegetables. We worked in weather that was warm and sometimes hot during spring and summer months, and rainy, windy and cool during the late fall and winter months.

Hence, the cans of kerosene were there to liven the smoldering fire in the heating stove. When we came into the bunk house at the end of a cold and rainy day, we were wearing metal hard hats, black woolen underwear, "tin" pants, held up by heavy duty suspenders and a "tin" jacket, and "cork" logger's boots. "Tin pants and jacket" were not made of tin. They were made of heavy water-proof canvas-like fabric, built to last. "Cork Logger's Boots," as well, were boots that had to be exceedingly well made to withstand the rigors of a logger's work as well as the severe rainy winter weather. The thick leather soles and heels had metal nail like inserts that would grab into the logs or the ground and thereby make walking on logs or ground more slip proof and safer.

Despite the water resistant qualities of our clothes and foot gear, we were not "soaking wet," but quite damp, and the heat felt good. If we would lift the lid on the heating stove just enough, so one could dump a whole gallon of kerosene on the smoldering fire, while quickly slamming down the heavy metal lid. The stove would then literally jump, vibrate and make roaring, explosive sounds inside its heavy metal covering, quickly warming up the old, wooden, railroad car, and its inhabitants.

The hearty meals were eaten in silence, lacking etiquette or the polite words of please, and thank you. Instead, "the boarding-house reach" came into being, with outstretched arms, nudging shoulders, with fingers pointing or grabbing at bowls and large plates. Breakfast started the day, with fried potatoes, bacon, sausages, pork chops, porridge, pan cakes, syrups, jellies and large metal pitchers containing hot, fresh, strong brewed black coffee to drink and to fill your thermos bottles for later in the day. Great food!

We rode the speeder out to our work place. Polson Logging Company used what they called "skyline logging" in that certain tall, sturdy trees were saved and left in a row extending out of sight to the back boundaries of a section that had been logged (trees cut down). A large pulley was installed at the top of each one of these trees.

A cable, starting from "the donkey engine" which was located next to the railroad track, went through each one of these large pulleys until it reached out to the back boundaries of the logged area. Other shorter cables with fasteners at the ends were attached to the main cable. These short cables were called chokers. Hence, the explanation of how the name for the man securing the chokers on logs that were laying on the ground came about, "choker setters." A "donkey engine" was a portable power unit used to winch logs from the forest to the central log pile, next to the railroad track. These "donkey engines" were portable, so, with their own power, they could be moved anywhere.

The distance from the area, where the logs were being dragged to the railroad track was variable. For communicating from the area to the operator of the "donkey engine" an electronic signal, called "the bug" was used. The "hook tender" (the foreman) would shout out a "hey" or "hey hey" or "hey hey hey" in a loud voice. A man called a "whistle punk" would usually be sitting on a stump (rarely standing), with " the bug" in his hand, that would transmit the hooktenders verbal "heys," into electronic sounds, from the back forest to the "donkey puncher" on his machine, next to the railroad track.

Chapter 52
George Wiley

The number of "heys" meant stop or go slow, or reverse direction or full speed and other designated orders. Our "hook tender" was George Wiley. George Wiley, a ruddy, well built man, in his early 60s. He was a seemingly displaced man because his vocabulary and mannerisms were out of place as a "hooktender in the tall timber."

Intermittently, his actions and projection suggested propriety, breeding and education. He appeared as if he would have been right at home, as an English planter on some distant, exotic island in the Caribbean Ocean in days gone by, or as a contemporary, corporate CEO in the business world. He had a way of using his vocabulary and mannerisms in projecting himself upward in the social structure. His excessive confidence was notable.

And George, as if he were an actor on stage, reversed his mannerisms. The proper language became salty and colorful, filled with four-letter words or terse, colorful statements tinged with anger. "Hey you, with a cow's breakfast on your head, grab a choker." He was addressing a "choker setter" who had been

Polson Loggin Co., Humptulips, WA.

Antilla & Alto Falling Team, WA.

slow to secure a choker around a log. Of course, "the cow's breakfast" was the straw hat he was wearing. The "chokersetters" wore whatever hat they owned. Other loggers were required to wear metal hard hats. Almost everyday, George would put on an "Academy Award Winning Performance" for us "choker setters," or anyone who happened to be there.

One time George Wiley became disturbed in the way the donkey puncher was responding to the signals "hey, hey, hey" that he, George was shouting to the "whistle punk." George told us "choker sitters" (his crew), "Stand aside. I have to train that varicose vein sonovabitch," on the "donkey engine" We knew George wanted more exactness, than he had been getting to his "hey-hey" commands. So we sat down and watched George.

For about five minutes, he shouted a mixture of "hey-heys" indicating stop, slow, reverse and full ahead with empty chokers dangling on the main cable. With the "whistle punk" sending George's signals to the unseen, but perhaps frustrated "donkey puncher" sitting on his machine by the distant railroad track. Finally, George stopped with the signals, with the remark, "Perhaps he will know how to run his machine now."

Another "hook tender" named Nick worked in the

area next to ours. He was Greek, and a friend of Nick's, a fellow Greek, worked as a choker setter in Nick's crew. His name was Steve. Both Greeks were grizzled, unshaven, and with dark complexions that caused them to look unwashed. Both spoke with a deep Greek accent, as if Ellis Island had been a recent stopping place.

Axel Carlson, the camp foreman, stopped by Nick's area one time when Nick was assisting the "donkey puncher" move his machine. Steve was standing by the machine.

Axel walked up and asked him in a contrasting Northern European Swedish sing-song accent," Vere is waat you call for da Nick?"

Steve replied, "He's under the donkey sunnovabeetch."

"Vaaat is he doing unter da donkey Steve?"

"Oh, he is sawing a stump bassturd."

"Tell Nick I vaant to see him," Axel said, also knowing that the expletives, "sonofabitch and basturd" were a part of Steve's English vocabulary and not intended to insult any person.

Chapter 53
Tree Topping

Later I went to Axel Carlson, the camp foreman, and told him that I was interested in other better paying jobs if there were ever any openings. He told me that there was one available as an apprentice to the camp tree topper. The tree topper topped tall, sturdy trees that would then be used like a mast on a ship is used, that is to install rigging on. These trees are then called "spar trees." Polson Camp Six and other large logging operations implemented what was then called "skyline logging," which involved dragging the logs in from outlying areas by chokers attached to a cable that run on the pulleys attached to the "spar trees."

Then inch and a quarter cables, attached to steel collars were secured on each "spar tree." The steel cables become guy lines, like on a ship's mast. Lastly, large pulleys were installed on the upper part of the trees. Countless huge logs could then be dragged to the landing next to the railroad tracks and then hauled to sawmills, paper mills and other places, where the logs were then converted into lumber, building products, and other uses. The tree topper cut the tops of these trees off, as well as rigged them.

Axel Carlson told me to report to Walter Wilson, the

camp tree topper and "spar tree rigger." Walter was of Finnish descent, a sturdy looking man. He appeared to be in late 70s, and remarkable physical condition. One of the many stories circulating in camp was that in past years, a large Finnish windjammer (sailing ship) had pulled into Seattle, Washington. And for one reason or another, the ship left Seattle without Walter Wilson.

Walter got employment in the tall timber of Washington and Oregon. The skills he had learned as a seaman, such as climbing a mast every night, in any kind of weather, and standing in the crow's nest, high above the rest of the ship, on look-out duty. He was skilled in tying various kinds of knots, splicing rope and steel cable. Many of these same skills, Walter discovered, were used by a tree topper and high climber.

I sought Walter out, and found a stoic Finn, and with an expression devoid of any emotion, he somberly said that Axel had already informed him of my apprenticeship. We would meet in the morning, and the training would begin. In the mornings, Walter and I got on a two-man motorized speeder that ran on railroad rails. We traveled to an isolated, heavily wooded area. This area would be logged in the near future.

Soon we parked our speeder, and headed for the
woods. I carried a topper's tools, attached to a sturdy
thick leather belt, to which was attached a rope. Walter
pointed out, that the rope had an interior steel cable
for a core for safety reasons. It was made this way
in case my ax hit the rope, instead of the tree. Also,
attached to the belt were two more ropes. One with an
ax attached to it, the other with a five foot long saw.

We walked into the woods, to a tree with the letter
X carved into the bark, about eye level. First Walter
had me put on the climbing cleats, one on each foot
and shoe. Next, I put the leather belt on. He showed
me how to toss the attached rope with my right hand
around the curvature of the tree and then how to grab
the end of the tossed rope with my left hand. Next, I
learned how to run the end of the rope through a steel
ring on my belt, pull the rope, leaving a little slack, and
then how to secure the rope on the steel ring with two
half-hitches.

Walter continued, "Take hold of the slack in the rope,
give one side an upward toss, and then the opposite
side an upward toss. Then dig one cleat into the tree
and climb upward, and then dig the other cleat into
the tree and climb upward. Repeat this, and you will
continue to get more slack in your rope, because the
tree is getting smaller, causing you to continually take
up the slack in the rope."

When in the upward climb, you were to get to a limb, then take your rope that is around the tree, loose from your belt. Take the end of the rope, and pass it over the limb, and secure the rope onto your belt again. Thus, the rope is on top of the limb. Next, saw the limb off. Continue doing this, until you get about 125 feet above the ground. Then you top the tree.

Walter continued, "Before you start chopping the undercut, take note in which direction the tree is leaning, and also, the winds direction, and how strong it is blowing." This is important for your own safety as well as having a sturdy, unsplintered top on the spar tree, instead of the possibility of experiencing a "barber chair." A "barber chair" topping is caused by a gusty wind or improper topping technique. The top of the tree will go over prematurely, splintering the bottom of the tree, and also making the top part of the bottom of the tree look roughly like a "barber chair," and unusable as a spar tree. When this happens, the vertical split on the upper part of the tree, will at the same time tighten the tree-topper's rope belt circling the tree, causing his death.

Chapter 54
One Heck of a Tree

Walter left the scene. I am not sure where he went, but he was not visible. Possibly he was sitting in the brush somewhere, watching. I started climbing the tree. When I got to a limb, I took the rope off my belt, held it in one hand, while with the other hand I put the end of the rope over the limb, secured the rope back on to my belt, and sawed the limb off.

I began to feel more confident, because everything was happening as it should. It was easy, so far. Then approximately, 100 feet up, a huge limb came into view. The limb was close to 18 inches in diameter. It had grown upward very close to the tree. Then it extended outward, away from the tree about thirty feet. The limb was large; it had grown in an awkward way, and it was noticeably heavy.

Wow, I don't know about this one. I thought of Walter's directions. Take the rope loose from your belt. Take the end of the rope in your other hand, and pass the end of the rope over the limb; secure the rope back on your belt. The rope is on top of the limb, cut the limb off.

I tried repeatedly and unsuccessfully to get the end of

Tree Topper, Polson Loging, WA.

the rope over the gnarled limb I took the rope loose from my belt, and attempted to hold to the rope with one hand, and take the very end of the rope in my other hand, and giving it a deliberate upward toss over the limb, but because of the largeness of the limb, and the awkward way that it had grown, I could not get the end of the rope over the limb, so that I could reach it with my loose hand. I was wet with sweat. My mouth was as dry as sand paper. My hands trembled as I was reaching for the end of the rope. The thought also passed into my consciousness of the distance of where I was to the ground—100 plus feet.

I thought, what would be the logical thing to do in this situation? Leave the rope as it is, under the limb, I decided. Undercut the limb from the bottom. That is chop and saw on the bottom of the limb. Then start sawing the limb from the top, until the limb dropped down. Because of the undercut, and the weight of huge branch, it should break loose from the tree, I surmised.

I sawed on the top of the limb, the weight caused the limb to drop down on my rope, but did not break off. I continued to chop and saw on the top of the limb. Unknown to me at the time, was that any limb, especially a large limb is attached to the whole tree, by strands that are grown into the core, not just fastened to the outer surface. Suddenly, the weight of the limb pulled a core and strands out of the inner part of the tree.

I felt the limb and me dropping downward about ten feet, pulling the core out of the tree with it, until the weight of the limb and the speed of its descent, tore the branch loose from the strands of the core, and fell to the ground. As I fell downward, the tree got bigger, causing my rope to tightened up, and at the same time pressing and burying my body and face into the bark of the tree.

The tightened rope saved my life and also kept me from any further descent. I loosened my rope enough, so I could dig my spurs into the tree, regain my dignity, and make my way downward to the ground. Once on the ground, I thought, I am not sure about this high climbing, tree topper business.

In the bunkhouse after supper, an older faller (timber faller), a fellow by the name of Waino Alto, approached me with a question, "How would you like to become a second faller?" He continued, "Lon Brooks, a North Carolina boy, has been my second faller for years, but he has now been approached by management to become a scaler." (A scaler is one who measures the trees and logs cut down or cut up by fallers or buckers every day.) Wow! I thought. A faller did not have the glamour of a "tree topper," but,

a faller was the highest paid of anyone in the camp.
I said yes, I would take the job of being his second
faller.

Chapter 55
Timber Faller's Work

The Timber Workers Union had forbidden the use of chainsaws in Gray's Harbor County, so all falling and cutting up of the timber was done by hand saws and axes.

Physical fitness was essential in becoming and being a faller. To cut a tree down, we would start out by chopping the undercut. An undercut is a wedge shaped piece chopped out of the side of the tree that is in the direction that the tree is going to fall. At times, the ground around a tree was uneven. For greater efficiency, and to make the chopping and sawing safer and easier, it was at times necessary for one or both fallers to use "spring boards." A spring board was an unplaned, five foot length of 2"x 6" plank, with a metal circular piece bolted to one end. A logger would chop a hole or holes into the tree, and then put the metal piece end of the board into the hole. The logger could then stand on the board and be at the same working level as his partner.

The faller's work was hard. However, the pay was excellent. Example: One day, we fell a huge cedar tree. Its dimensions: the base of the tree was seven feet by eleven feet. It took a half a day to chop the undercut in, and about ninety minutes to saw the tree down. In falling trees, we try to prevent the falling tree from hitting any stumps or objects that would break the tree. We were earning from forty to one hundred dollars a day, each. In comparison, a "chocker sitter was being paid approximately sixteen dollars a day."

Friday completed the work week. One could stay in camp and read, rest, do your laundry and visit with the other "stay at camp" men. Or go to town, home to families, or as some loggers chose to do, "serious drinking." One of the more popular "logger bars," was the "Wirta Hotel" in Aberdeen. A triangular-shaped bar to lean against and old friends as well as new acquaintances to drink with made the day and night pleasurable.

A few drinks, old friends and friendly surroundings bring out the congeniality in people, especially loggers. So in a "logging country" bar, one occasionally hears the animated word shouted in a loud voice, "Timber," which means and is interpreted by the bartender and everyone else in the bar that the person doing the shouting is going to buy everyone a drink. After a few more drinks, warm feelings, and hard-earned wages being spent, setting up drinks for "the house," the word "Timber" was repeatedly voiced by others.

I worked a year as a "timber faller" in the "rain forest" of Washington, as it was called. I found a similarity between a logger's life and the life of a seaman. Drinking and the things that went with it did not have a long-term appeal. I thought, perhaps, going back to sea, or perhaps sailing on the Great Lakes as a seaman, had more stability, and upward career mobility, so I went back to Minnesota and the sailor's life.

Chapter 56
The Great Lakes and a Wedding

I sailed on The Great Lakes for three years as a wheelsman. The ships I sailed on loaded iron ore in Duluth or Two Harbors, Minnesota. We would then haul our cargo to the eastern Great Lakes, unload and then repeat the process—back to the Lake Superior ports, load up with iron ore and back to the Eastern ports that were near the blast furnaces, where the raw iron ore would be converted to steel and steel products.

Meanwhile, my relationship with Berdie Wivell had progressed, and we set a wedding date. Our plans were to have me take off a trip, which was one week, and then I would continue sailing as a wheelsman, write for my third mate's license and then progress up the ladder to second mate, first mate and finally Captain.

Chapter 57
Underground Miner

Things did not work out that way. That one week off the ship included a lot of conversation about the present as well as future years. We decided that perhaps a job on shore would be a wiser choice. So we turned our thoughts to finding a job for me. I heard that an underground iron ore mine was hiring in Ely, Minnesota. I went to the mine and the hiring rumors were true. I was hired immediately, and became a laborer and "spare miner" at 1,700 feet underground level in the Pioneer Mine.

Working in an underground mine, was indeed a new experience. The clothing was the same for everyone, rubber-steel toed boots, bib overalls and a jacket. A specially designed hard hat had an attached light. A cable ran from the light to a catalog size battery that was attached to a thick leather belt. The miner wore the belt, with attached battery, over all his clothes.

At the end of the shift, a miner would turn in his light, belt and battery. They would be recharged, so at the beginning of each of the three shifts, a miner would strap on a freshly charged battery and light. The lights, hard hats, clothing and the faces of the men that wore them, had that worn look, a look that suggested a life of hard work, inward strength and a nobility of a sort.

The means used to get the miners into the depths and bowels of the earth was called "the cage." It was a crude-looking platform with a heavy metal wire around the four sides. The men were working at four elevations and the 1700 ft. level was the bottom. The men were jostled and packed in, so that all the space was efficiently used. Being a mining town with diverse ethnicity, Ely was made up of families from throughout Europe.

The miners were aware of the closeness in "the cage," and the kind of food that had been recently consumed during the miner's off-shift hours, for the close proximity was alive with earthy, garlicky and pungent flavors, and occasionally, repulsive odors of a different kind. The fast descent and the knee shaking stops to the 1700 ft. level were taken in stride, as a way of life. They were old-time veterans of underground mining, with an occasional tender-foot like me.

I worked with two miners of Slavic origin, Matt Baudek and Tony Mikolich. Both of them were in their 60s or older. The Slavs seemed to have a great sense of humor, with laughter a part of every conversation. We did a variety of work, cleaning ditches, piling logs and lumber. Our work area received illumination from the lamps on our hard hats. I was also categorized as a "spare miner." A "spare miner" went mining ore, when a miner was on vacation or when a miner did not show up for work.

I looked forward to being assigned as a "spare miner" because my pay increased, and I had the opportunity to learn more about mining methods, and perhaps through attrition or for some other reason, a vacancy would develop, and I would have the opportunity to mining steady.

One day, the foreman informed me that I was to go "raise mining" with Kelly. Raise mining was drilling a shaft upward, to the next level. Kelly and I climbed a makeshift ladder 34 feet, to a platform that was resting on timbers that had been laid "log cabin style." Our excavation was approximately six feet by six feet. We drilled for days on our shift. The other miners drilled on the other two shifts. It so turned out that when the drilling was completed, Kelly and I had the work of filling the drilled holes with dynamite and blasting on our shift.

We carried several boxes of dynamite and fuse to our work platform. We had approximately one hundred holes, six feet deep, to fill with dynamite. After the holes were filled, Kelly explained to me the pattern that he wanted to use to get an efficient blast. The fuses were dangling downward from the ceiling. They had to be lit with a lighter shaped like pencil with an inner string like fuse. A lighter first had to be lit with a match.

"Start by lighting the center holes first, so that they would be the first to explode. Then work outward to the outer holes." He also told me that after seven or eight minutes we would not be able to see each other because of the smoke from the burning fuses.

He continued, "So you will have to feel for the unlit fuses, for in them, there is no heat. When your part of the fuses are lit, make your way to the ladder and get out of here, carefully but quickly." I did that, and Kelly followed shortly.
We got out of the area and waited. In about ten minutes, multiple blasts started going off. An underground blast is extremely loud because the sound of the blast ricochets into all the cavities. The area filled with smoke, powder smell and dust, a good time for a lunch break while the air cleared itself out.

In 1952, the work contract between the men and the union expired. I had heard that a new taconite plant was being constructed at Silver Bay, and there was work available. I went there and obtained construction work that lasted three years. Afterwards,

I obtained a permanent job with Reserve Mining Company that lasted 27 years, the first 13 years in the Maintenance Department, the last 14 years in the Industrial Engineering Department. During this time, I went to night school at the University of Minnesota Duluth. After seven years, I was awarded a four-year BA degree in English Literature.

Chapter 58
Life With Berdie

I purchased almost eight acres at Little Marais and we lived there 52 years. We raised three sons, and started three businesses. We did this as an extra sideline, with Berdie, my wife, doing most of the work. A negative factor in our business as well as our personal family life, was our briny, saltwater wells. Drilling two wells was costly. Both of them, salt water. The water could not be used in cooking. Washing your body with salt water is difficult. The salt water is so hard that the soap does not suds up. A disappointment indeed.

Our first business was a summer drive-in food business. We ran this business five years. The business was successful, but not successful enough. We closed the business and took the summers off. We went camping, biking and traveling with our three sons, Dean, Joe and Scott. We had an enjoyable time. The boys were growing and learning to become great adults.

The turbulent 1960s and the early 1970s were a time period that encompassed Viet Nam, changing values in a changing world. Our sons were busy with Cub Scouts, Boy Scouts, piano lessons, Sunday school lessons, as well as school lessons. We cross-country skied in the winter and bicycled during the summer. It was fun and a recreation that was affordable The boys were busy. One by one they graduated and left home and pursued schooling, jobs, and travel. We are proud and grateful that all three sons are successful, healthy and happy.

Our next business was a photography studio. I was introduced to photography at work in the Industrial Engineering Department at Reserve Mining. On one of my vacations, I went to a professional photography school in Indiana. The photography business went quite well, photographing weddings, graduations, families and occasionally newspaper photos. We used our upstairs bedroom for backdrops, camera lights and various tripods. Berdie, my wife, took care of the negatives, scheduling and billing. Berdie also framed pictures and assisted in photographic applications.

**Scott, Joe and Dean waiting
for the school bus.**

Chapter 59
Two Gift Shops

After much conversation and thought, we decided that the gift shop business would be less stressful, more enjoyable and more profitable. Why not take a chance? So we closed the photography business and Berdie started "The Scandinavian House." It was a success and fun from the start. I wanted signs for our business that were different. I came up with a design that was made with newly sawed rough wooden planks glued together. The many rough planks became a singular, massive piece of wood. I sanded the wood and cut the sides in a wavy, irregular pattern.

Berdie sketched the outline of large letters into the words, ANTILLA'S GIFTS, which I routered out, and painted black. I then brushed on a transparent liquid sealer, further enhancing the raw, wood look. The finished sign was superb! I made about six of them. One was eight feet by twenty four feet. Customers and other people were photographing and initiating conversation about them, so I knew that I had a winner.

The signs stopped cars and customers. The parking lot was massive, yet it was full continually. Cars left

Antilla's Gifts, Little Marais, MN.

Antilla's Gifts, Little Marais, MN.

Franks' shop, "The Barn".

Berdies Shop, "The Scandia House".

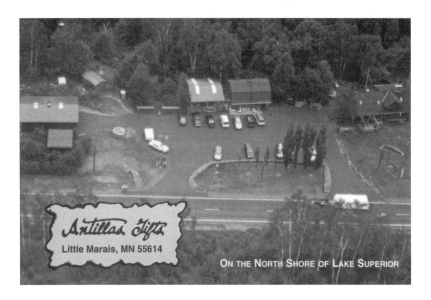

Antillas Gifts
Little Marais, MN 55614

ON THE NORTH SHORE OF LAKE SUPERIOR

loaded with gifts. Satisfaction after the purchases were not empty words, because over the years, most returned repeatedly and friendships with our customers developed. We traveled to distant wholesalers and to Europe to maintain quality and uniqueness. To stay away from the sameness of other shops, Berdie and I purchased upscale gifts and a variety of them. Her single gift shop was packed with quality gifts of every sort, and people were buying.

In 1982, the Reserve Mining Company shut down, and I was laid off work. It was an easy decision for Berdie and I to make, build another gift shop. Our builder, Erkki Harju, was a recent immigrant from Finland and was joined by his son John, and another carpenter, Ed Dettweiler.

Erkki was a man who was competent in many skills. I told him I wanted a Scandinavian barn with heavy timbers throughout the building and other details. They built the barn, and like the signs, the barn was colorful. The design suggested a northern European flavor and the resulting building was exceptional. Using skills I had learned as a sailor, rope splices, knots, yellow manila rope and shelves made out of heavy wood, sanding, transparent wood sealer, sweat, tears and hope, and we had a new building, waiting to be filled with gift items.

We went to gift shows in the U.S., and made several trips to Europe where we rented a car in Germany and traveled. We purchased gift items in Finland, Sweden, Norway and Denmark. We were ready.

We ran our business for 25 years. The money was rolling in, beyond our expectations, and the cash was accumulating. I remembered my old first mate and friend, George Smith, and our time on a harbor tugboat in Europe during WW II. He had talked to my buddy Dave Farrel and me about "getting ahead in life."

He told us that the way to do it was through learning and investing in the stock market. Many discussions held at random times on our ship, about "ordinary sailor talk" turned to "investment talk." Perhaps it was because of the hunger to get ahead, that lay within; a hunger that gave rise to the hope that it was possible to improve one's economic status.

I thought, well the logical way to learn about investing, stocks and Wall Street would be to join an investment club, which I did. I was introduced to investment publications that our club used for creditable references, discussion and purchase of specific stocks. Daily, the stock market page became priority reading. Using investment club discussion and stock buying picks, as well as the results obtained from such picks, became my own investment format. Success fired up our motivation, and also my silent gratitude to our investment discussions with George Smith.

Chapter 60
Lake Superior is Not For Sissies

Our success in business prompted me to think seriously about spending some money on one of my interests, sailing and sailboats. I had pushed the thought away from my consciousness time and again. But now things were different. Maybe we could get serious and buy one. We talked about it; we rehashed it. We decided yes, we will buy a sailboat. We bought a small one; one which we promptly traded for a bigger one; then another one. We enjoyed having a boat immensely; however, I was still thinking of a bigger and better sailboat.

Ever since I helped rig up a makeshift jury mast on our training ship's lifeboat in Seattle during my Merchant Marine training days back in 1943, my interest and enjoyment in sailing has grown. Our instructor—an old salt and one of my seaman's school class mates—and I sailed around Puget Sound. What a day, no motor, just the wind and sails.

One day, when Berdie and I were driving to Duluth, and as usual we were looking at "the lake." While we have lived next to Lake Superior for a bunch of years, it still gets our attention. I have never had an infatuation with Lake Superior. I have found it unfriendly, aggressive, threatening and unforgiving. "The lake" is like a boy in my grade school years. Because of his size, he would pound, threaten, and intimidate you as he wanted.

I like bodies of water, because of the recreation possibilities, as well as the aesthetic value. But Lake Superior has an ominous flavor. Several years ago, I made a Lake Superior crossing in a 22' sailboat, unknowingly in nice weather that developed into a storm. But now I am getting ahead of myself.

We heard of a British-made boat for sale in Wisconsin. One wintry Sunday, we drove to Bayfield to look at this boat. There it was, sitting in a cradle, all wrapped up in canvas and rope, like a cocoon.

I untied the rope, pushed back the canvas, and crawled into the boat with a flashlight. I could see the interior construction, the galley, the head (the toilet), and the sleeping quarters. I was overwhelmed with the beauty and the workmanship of this European-made boat. It had to be mine.

The winter passed quickly and in May, Berdie drove me to Bayfield and she then returned home. I quickly had the boat into the water, lines, sails checked over, and the interior of the cabin clean and shipshape.

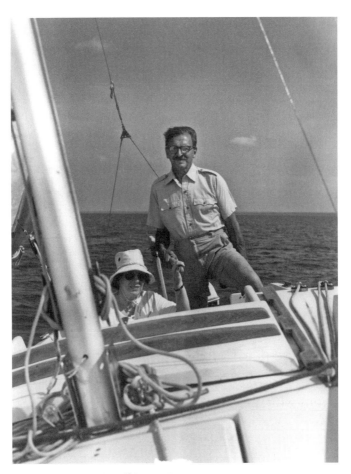

Sailing Partners.

I secured the tiller and walked forward and pulled on the line that raised the mainsail. Immediately, the boat lurched over, and then steadied and we were moving. Thrilling! Chunks of ice floated by the boat. There was the feel of a promising frigid wind on my face and with the sound of hungry seagulls surveying the water below for food. The ambience seemed to be reminiscent of one's primal past.

I then raised the jib sail (the most forward and smallest sail). I could feel the increased acceleration. The boat quickly gained speed and acquired a rhythmic roll and an occasional unexpected pitch. The movement of the boat, the changing intensity of the wind and the occasional cold spray, kept one's mind on the job and also brought back memories of my Merchant Marine days during WW II.

Slapping sounds ensued from the sails, when the wind shifted or when the boat was changing its angle when tacking. The smooth, sensual rustling sounds when the wind pressure was constant. The sails quietly did their work. The limited movement of the mast and the boom created a restful, creaking sound with same cadence as the roll of the ship. No telephone, no TV, no meaningless conversations, and the feel of the vibrations of the water passing under the hull completed the ambience of being underway in a sailboat.

Late afternoon, I tied up to an old fisherman's wharf on Sand Island. I prepared my supper on a mariner's alcohol stove. The heat from the stove and the two candles I had burning for illumination warmed up the cabin. The rising wind was creating a rolling sea, which would slam into the dock and onto the tied up boat. In my warm and cozy cabin, I could hear the outside sound of water running off the boat's cabin down into the self bailing cockpit. With the sailboat pressed up against the dock, and the rhythmic beating of the empty sail lines and the other halyards against the mast, the thrilling realization came to me, that my "lake crossing" was well on its way.

In the morning, I set sail. I noticed a freshening wind, with the waves further apart. The sails were full, with the boat heeling over more. Logic told me that the wind could increase more, accompanied by more difficulty with sail handling. I decided to drop the main sail and to just use the jib. A smart move because the wind became intense. I locked the cabin door, in case the boat was knocked down, it would still float. I had on rubber boots, oilskins, and a "southwestern" on my head. The water would surge into the cockpit, and at times it was between my knees and crotch.

Two Harbors soon turned up, and I changed course to Knife River.

My friend Fred and Berdie were there waiting. Their faces revealed their relief, for with their binoculars they had seen a small boat, with a handkerchief of a sail, on a storm-tossed lake and they were not sure who was going to win out. It was a great trip, and a wonderful boat. We have traded boats two more times since "the Lake crossing." Presently, we have an 18 foot sloop, two years old. It is trailerable, so no marina fees. Sailing continues to be our favorite pass time. We are grateful for the good times summer brings.

Chapter 61
Further Along Life's Journey

We sold our business and our property at Little Marais in January 2003. Berdie and I are both aware that we are getting further along on life's journey. In fact, I am getting to the end of writing, my "life story." The worlds of which I have written are no longer there. In my memories, they will remain a part of me.

The decks of ships where I have walked, the feel of the wooden steering wheel in my hands, with the fancy knot work on the top spoke, so that in the darkness of the night watches, as well as by day, feeling the knot work on that certain spoke, told me the position of the ship's rudder. I remember the cold dampness of fog on my face, while standing the dark, lonely, lookout watches.

I remember the distinct smell of oilskins (rain gear) when entering our cabin, or "focsul" on older ships. I can still see the lighted docks at night and hear the querulous shouts of the longshoremen getting our holds packed with assorted cargo. The unforgettable sound of the deep-throated blast of our ship's whistle, as we back out of the dock, still brings on memories of a steamer and crew, adventure bound to far away places.

I remember hearing the pelting rain on my metal hard hat, and the towering trees over my head, and the sound of them crashing to the ground when my partner Waino Alto and I were tree fallers in "The Rain Forest" of Washington state.

I remember the underground miner's job, where any mistakes had fatal possibilities. I remember the efficiency and camaraderie of Reserve Mining Company's maintenance crew. I remember the praise as well as the stinging criticism of a competent boss in the Industrial Engineering Department. Memories, yes, lots of them.

I am grateful to be here and write the story.

Lessons that have helped me

1. Make or take time to pray.

2. Read more books than you did last year.

3. Don't compare your life to others. You have no idea what their journey is about.

4. Don't have negative thoughts on things you cannot control. Instead invest your energy in the positive present moment.

5. Forget issues of the past. Don't remind your partner of his/her mistakes of the past. That will ruin your present happiness.

6. No one is in charge of your happiness except you.

7. Realize that life is a school and you are here to learn.

8. Each day, give something good to others.

9. Forgive everyone for everything.

10. What other people think of you is none of your business.

11. God heals everything.

12. No matter how you feel, get up, dress up and show up.

13. Save a part of what you earn.

14. Join an investment club.

15. The best is yet to come.

16. When you awake alive in the morning, thank God for it.

17. Associate with the noblest people you can find.

18. Read the best books.

19. Live with the mighty, but learn to be happy alone.

20. Rely on your own energies, and don't wait or depend on others.

21. Life shrinks or expands in proportion to one's courage.

22. Join a Toastmaster's Club.

Frank and Berdie Antilla
Married – 59 Years.

Left Home at Sixteen

Book Order

"LEFT HOME AT 16"
by Frank Antilla

_____

Name

_____

Address

_____

City State Zip

_____ copies: To order, send $20.95 ($15.95 + $5.00 S&H)

_____ **TOTAL**

Make check or money order to:
Frank Antilla
P.O. Box 24
Two Harbors, MN 55616

Please indicate if you want the book autographed and
to whom_____

Books will be mailed 2 to 3 weeks from order date.